"This is the most important environmental book of the decade [1989]."
  —W. David Laird, *Books of the Southwest*

"Hey, this is the real shit."
  —the late, great Galen Rowell, photographer and author

"It's something we all feel qualified to do, yet never talk about . . .
For once, we get good tips on how to keep campsites clean while
maintaining modesty and comfort."
  —*Outside*

"Doesn't take the reader long to get used to THAT word, or to concede that the well-prepared book is a critical woodcraft manual."
  —Lee Straight, *BC Outdoors*

"Meyer's little book should be essential reading for everyone who
goes into the outdoors. It should be given to everyone who takes
part in any outdoors adventure course and it should be on the
curriculum of every school where outdoor education is taught."
  —Cameron McNeish, www.cameronmcneish.co.uk

"This well-written little manual deals factually and honestly with
all the problems of personal sanitation in the out-of-doors."
  —Robert Fulghum, *Seattle Times*

"There is no easy way to say this: You have to learn how to properly
defecate in the woods. . . . Fortunately, former river guide Kathleen
Meyer is less squeamish than the rest of us, and has written an
authoritative and entertaining book."
  —*USA Today*

"Meyer leaves no stones unturned explaining the dos and don'ts
of proper excretory techniques."
  —Roger Vargo, www.4x4now.com

"The ultimate title in the genre."
  —*Penthouse*

D0289585

"This is a *great* book! I wholeheartedly agree with Ms. Meyer's
environmental concerns. . . ."
  —Linda Svendsen, director, Boojum Expeditions

HOW TO SHIT
IN THE WOODS

An environmentally sound
approach to a lost art

Kathleen Meyer

TEN SPEED PRESS
Berkeley

Published in the United States by Ten Speed Press, an imprint of the
Crown Publishing Group, a division of Random House, Inc., New York.
www.crownpublishing.com
www.tenspeed.com

Ten Speed Press and the Ten Speed Press colophon are registered
trademarks of Random House, Inc.

Cover photo, foreground, by Bill Schwab Photography;
background by Kent & Charlene Krone / Purestock / SuperStock
Illustration on page ii by Pedro Gonzalez
Chapter opening illustrations by J. S. McVey
"Poop Tube" illustration on page 67 by John Larson

Library of Congress Cataloging-in-Publication Data
Meyer, Kathleen
 How to shit in the woods : an environmentally sound approach
to a lost art / Kathleen Meyer. — 3rd ed.
     p. cm.
 Includes bibliographical references and index.
 1. Mountaineering—Health aspects—Handbooks, manuals, etc. 2.
Defecation—Handbooks, manuals, etc. I. Title.
 RC1220.M6M48 2011
 613.6—dc22
                                2010020819

 ISBN 978-1-58008-363-8 (alk. paper)

Third edition

Design by Colleen Cain
Printed in the United States

10 9 8 7 6 5 4 3 2 1

In tribute to Father and his unorthodox ways;
he would have approved of this subject.

In memory of Uncle Ernie,
the only other rebel-writer in the family,
who inspired and delighted me with his letters
for so many years.

In fond remembrance of Suzanne Lipsett
and dear Phil Wood.

Always for my Patricio.

Contents

Acknowledgments

Someone recently said, "This is the shortest book with the longest acknowledgments." That it is, and lengthening with each edition. Yet the biggest bulk of contributors are not even mentioned. The chapters that follow emerged through the course of my collecting stories that generically belong to many. What else can I say?

A quick look at the list below brings home to me the emotional airlift it took to become a first-time author with shit for a subject. Untold thanks go out to the following people:

Jon Runnestrand, who never failed to reaffirm my choice of untrodden paths, reminding me to—above all else in the face of disaster—keep rowing!

Mark DuBois and Marty McDonnell, who, many years ago, gently straightened out my city ways by presenting me with a healthy dose of respect for Mother Nature and offering me the first clues as to what were the real and simple joys in life. And Mark for his contributions and careful editing of the first edition and help with the third.

Craig Reisner for further heightening my sensitivities to human impact. Rick Spittler for hours of environmental brainstorming and a long, dear friendship.

Howard Backer, M.D., for editing the *Giardia* section in the first edition, supplying updates for the second and information for third.

Bruce and Suzanne Degan for their encouragement, dinners, and computer. And Michael Fahey for his special and supporting friendship.

My treasured women friends, who hold me up through all the nutziness of life's daily turmoil: Carol Newman, Joanne Solberg, Katya Merrell, Linda Cunningham, Jan Reiter, Carolee Wilson, Lizzie Young, Susan Adams, Fredi Bloom, Joyce Ciemny, Barbara Gordon, Martha Beecher, Ellen Davidson, Martha Massey, and Jennie Shepard.

My very first woman friend, my precious liberated mother, for believing in me and in this subject when she was ninety years old.

Darling Jean Hayes for the blessings of clarity and the freedom to become.

Edith Bond and her late husband, Fred, and Frank and Ronita Egger for standing in as family.

The late Silvio Piccinotti for his wonderful old stories and generous ways and teaching me to drive draft horses; our mornings clopping down the road kept me grounded and sane through writing the original manuscript and then prepared me for the next evolution in my life.

Suzanne Lipsett, who is always in my heart as an ace friend and editor.

Sal Glynn—the man who might have become a great saucier, had he not ended up a superior editor.

Veronica Randall, who not only rendered her unparalleled editorial expertise at full tilt boogie but donned, agiley, the old farm harness and away we went—a galloping team.

Copyeditor Karen Levy for her welcome sharp eye.

Robert Stricker, my agent and a dear man, for beating down my door and making everything happen and happen and happen. And Ten Speed Press and Crown Books and Random House for a thoroughly enjoyable publishing experience.

Countless others who offered encouragement, direction, inspiration, instruction, or life support. To name a few, some here and some gone but vivid in memory: Connie Thomas, Bruce Raley, Robert Volpert, Bonnie Evans, Norm Frankland, Art Schmedt, Susan Still, Catherine Fox, Esther Young, Stephen McDade, and Cameron Macdonald.

In celebration of life: Georgia Milan, Daniel Braby, William Nichols, Kathy Markette, David Bellamah, Jim and Joan Hintz, Glen and Dottie Johnshoy, David and Renée Breeden, Ron White, Frank Ringel and Patricia Doyle, Ben and Carrie Short, Scott and Laurie Davidson, Bob and Adrian Marshall, Jean Meneley, Russell Smart, Jeannie Warner, Patti Jo Thomas, Glen Gilmore, Mike and Denise Mollè, Peg Klouda and Brian Cherry, Bill LaCroix and Amy Sage, Chris and Marina Weatherly, Sash and Mary and Jim and Ken, Andy and Sarah Roubik, Michael Helling, Amy Kraft, Mike McEachern, Nancy Boice, Rod Norum, Roger Ahern, Deirdre Boggs, and Larry Draper.

The Indiana family: Bill and Sandy Robbins.

Phil and Julie, Nick, and Dexter—could never, *ever* have done it without you.

All those helpful folks—largely voices without faces—at the Environmental Protection Agency, Centers for Disease Control and Prevention, U.S. Forest Service, Bureau of Land Management, National Park Service, numerous sanitary districts, San Anselmo Public Library, U.C. Medical Library, Missoula Public Library, St. Patrick's Medical Library, and the Maureen and Mike Mansfield Library. Especially, Bob Abbott, LuVerne Grussing, Roger Drake, and Baird Beaudreau.

And not least: Lenore Anderson, Joshua Cole, Tyler Fish, and Jenessa Conner at Colorado Outward Bound; Rich Brame and Haven Holsapple at the National Outdoor Leadership School; Jen Lamb and Ben Lawhon at the Leave No Trace Center for Outdoor Ethics. Dr. Charles Helm, Donald Studer, Charlie Mabbot, Bill Goslin, Shirley Volger Meister, Therese Plair, Erick Hendricksen, and Walt Luebeck. All at what used to be Marin Outdoors. In Missoula, at The Trailhead, Jason Kauffman; at Pipestone Mountaineering, Dave Kratochvil; and at Recreational Equipment, Inc. (REI), Sean Pascoe. Brian Oram at Wilkes University Center for Environmental Quality, Environmental Engineering, and Earth Sciences; David Rootes, director of Antarctic Logistics and Expeditions; Roger Robinson, Chief Mountaineering Ranger at Denali National Park and Preserve; and Ellen Lapham at the American Alpine Club.

Also, the many who have written to or emailed me (there has been no shortage of eagerness to comment on this subject). You will find much of the information incorporated into this third edition.

Finally, of course, I'm indebted to everyone who so unabashedly shared a worst shit story knowing that it would be spread before the world. You know who you are; I won't mention any names.

🌱

As this book goes to print, news has reached me about the untimely death of James "Walkin' Jim" Stoltz. In tribute to him, please take a quiet moment to bask in the wealth of inspiration and goodness he brought to this planet.

I dyde shyte thre grete toordes.
　　—*Fables of Aesop*, Caxton Translation, Vol. 15, 1484

Thou shalt have a place also without the camp, where thou shalt go forth abroad: And thou shalt have a paddle upon thy weapon; and it shall be when thou shalt ease thyself abroad, thou shalt dig therewith, and thou shalt turn back, and cover that which cometh from thee.
　　—Deuteronomy 23:12–13

Third Edition Preface

With *How to Shit in the Woods* coming into its against-all-odds, twenty-first year of life, I've begun to think of it as finally legal—amazing even myself. When long ago I set about scribbling the first chapter, everyone but a few friends had counseled that "shit" would be no word for a cover, no word for a bookstore window—I should title it *When Nature Calls.* "Too blah," I'd muttered, "too esoteric." Then, in fact, numerous publishers refused to touch the manuscript, as if it off-gassed whiffles of the real stuff. Even divisions of Random House (who, in a bit of irony, have recently acquired the rights) all passed on it. But driven, as I was, by the sight of desecrated beaches and woodland paths over sixteen years of guiding whitewater rafting trips, and with no background in writing, the voice that kept bubbling up from within was one of directness. My mission, as it were, became to haul this taboo topic into the light of day. (Nuances of my original struggle with terminology and title are discussed in the Author's Note.)

As it turned out, when finally in print, the guide in all its shitty glory shot out the gate at the Frankfurt Book Fair, running away with *Bookseller* magazine's prize for "Oddest Book Title of the Year," and the next thing I knew—well, nearly—it had become a training aid for the respectable likes of scout troops, outdoor schools, and inner city wilderness programs; for rangers with the U.S. Forest Service, National Park Service, and Bureau of Land Management; for whitewater rafting guides; and for members of the military. Seven languages later now, sales have passed 2.5 million. Word filters back that copies have been spotted gracing a library shelf at McMurdo Station, Antarctica; selling in a country store north of the Arctic Circle; bedecking a bookstore in South Africa and a B&B in Scotland. *How to Shit* has traveled the world—from South Africa to Zimbabwe, to New Zealand, Australia, Malaysia, Japan, Canada's Northwest Territories, Ireland, Scotland, England, Denmark, Poland, Spain, France,

Germany, Estonia, Slovenia, and India. Since that blustery December day in 1989, when Phil Wood and George Young at Ten Speed Press committed to unveiling—front and center—a scatological expletive, squatting down to shit in this ol' world hasn't been the same.

Because of the scandalous nature of the title, with the first printing, Ten Speed's clever marketing department offered a choice in covers: the one you hold now and a rendition with a bleeped-out scatological expletive, *how to s--- in the woods*, its lowercase black lettering set on a green sprig of mountain maple against (I've always thought) a rather pee-yellow background. Yet, from title pages onward, identical books. *Let the public decide where their sensibilities lie!* And decide they rapidly did.

In 1993, a federal multi-agency task force, bearing the appellation Human Waste Management of Federal Lands, was set up to probe the problem and raise awareness. LuVerne Grussing of Idaho's Bureau of Land Management (BLM) directed the effort. I spoke to Grussing that year, in preparation for my second edition, but it wasn't until 2010, when I looked him up again, that I heard the entire story. The task force had grown inadvertently out of a river trip. Cy Jamison, then BLM's national director, was on that trip and happened, at its end, to witness the group's carefully bagged-up excrement being slipped into the dumpster of a country store. (This was the ugly gap in disposal I'd written about in my first edition, suggesting that the U.S. Forest Service might be the entity to address it.) Participants in the task force made an impressive group indeed: the U.S. Forest Service, BLM, National Park Service, U.S. Fish & Wildlife, Bureau of Reclamation, Environmental Protection Agency, and, of all things, NASA, who had their own poo puzzlements.

Meanwhile, the very subject of bodily eliminations leapt onto the charming plain of children's books: *Everyone Poops,* by Japanese author Taro Gomi; *The Gas We Pass: The Story of Farts,* by Japanese author Shinta Cho; and, adorable, *The Story of the Little Mole Who Went in Search of Whodunit* [Who, pray tell, pooped on his head?], by German author Werner Holzwarth. And this, of course, is where all successful movements need to begin, with the wee ones.

Then one morning, my fax machine spewed out a page with this bold letterhead: **Japan Toilet Association**. *A practical joke from a ribald friend?* Rather, an official invitation—below which flowed the hand-brushed character of one Secretary General Koo Ue—to follow *Shit*'s Japanese translation to Toyama, on the Sea of Japan, and deliver a keynote address at the third International Toilet Symposium/Expo, headlined "Toilets and the Environment, 1996." The event's 28 countries and 800 attendees marked the first major gathering to examine problems of human waste management in (oxymoron that it is) high-use wilderness. My interpreters whisked me off on the train to Unazuki, the hot springs resort town where a tramway carries hikers high into the Japan Alps. The next morning, I spoke to 150 keepers of the mountains, sharing the latest in techniques for packing-it-out. Japan is to be roundly applauded for spearheading a worldwide bathroom-and-sanitation revolution. A small study group who called themselves Toiletopia had been meeting for fifteen years when they founded JTA, in 1985, and adopted the ambitious goal to make safe, keep clean, and beautify Japan's public toilets. And then the world's.

The practice of packing-it-out looms large again in this edition. Whitewater boaters, sea kayakers, and cavers—long the stars—have been joined by hunters, four-wheelers, backpackers, canoeists, and big wall climbers. But leading the herd in twenty-first-century packing-it-out (with concerns about aesthetics, sanitation, disease, and pollution) are mountaineers. In July 2010, the American Alpine Club hosted the conference "Exit Strategies: Managing Human Waste in the Wild" at the American Mountaineering Center in Golden, Colorado. It was the first international conference of its kind in the U.S., and twelve countries were in attendance. I felt nothing but humbled and privileged to find myself among a group with such passion and dedication. All the conference presentations will become available online. Look to my website for the links (www.KathleenintheWoods.net).

In our heavily trafficked wild areas—be they places of jumping waters or serpentine trails, snowy slopes or rocky terrain—the prevailing shift is toward regulated packing-it-out. To hear of a charmed soul taking care of her own leavings, willingly (minus rules), always warms my heart. Ponder this: Are we a species willing to clip a small container of excreta to our backpacks, or are we more an animal prone to paying taxes for wilderness police? Airport security at every trailhead?

And then, I believe we have one more step, a tough one perhaps. To discuss it, I propose we step out into the sunshine.

Climate crises are upon us, everywhere. Each season turning more radical, more violent. The earth, scientists say, is headed toward regions of drastic wet and dry. Within these pages, you'll meet Kevin McCoy and Kevin Hoskins of Oregon's BLM, who have dry toilet futures pretty well figured out—all but the final *composting*. For that, help is here in the form of a book we all ought to be reading, the *Humanure Handbook: A Guide to Composting Human Manure* by Joseph

Jenkins (www.josephjenkins.com). A friendly scientific treatise, it's based on thirty-five years of raising a family of six children on a household waterless bucket system, each deposit covered with a scoop of sawdust—or, if you don't live among Pennsylvania hardwoods, then something on the order of peat moss or rice hulls. Year after year, the Jenkins' cured humanure—with its pathogens baked out; with no plastic bags; no chemical powders; no municipal sewer toxins; no fuel expenditure (but for a once-a-week stroll outside to empty a bucket or two); no big expense; and, best of all, no odor—is transferred from its elegant backyard bin, the Humanure Hacienda, to the family's organic vegetable garden and orchard. Recently, Jenkins has been teaching humanure composting in Haiti, helping in the aftermath of the earthquake. His mantra: "Human *waste* is a thing of the past."

Was that a laugh? Or a whimper? Well then, cut it out! It's with waterless toilet systems that we'll have a chance of preserving enough clean, fresh water for the essentials of drinking, cooking, and washing. And there's nothing to stop us from carrying this practice into the backcountry, with composting sites near trailheads and take-outs.

Come to find out, my blind groping to report on this subject, to offer permission to talk out loud about it, has been of some help, although I can't claim all the credit for instigating modern casual potty talk. Long before me, people were mulling over the accumulation problem. Today, many others tote the load. Still, with my fairly well having owned the written subject and worn the moniker "Shit Lady" for nigh on a third of my life, I *revel* in the company and reassurance that it's not just my mind that's startlingly awash in whizzing and crapping matters. A steadily rising global consciousness is a delight to behold.

Lamentably, the story of shitting in the woods is not finished. The fouling of our precious little backcountry, highest peaks, and sunniest beaches is a plague by no means wholly remedied. Reports of revile flood back to me. Sewage yet flows into streets, rivers, and seas. Here at home, wilderness rangers tell of encountering human excrement strung all over campsites. And evermore far-flung, pristine corners of the globe keep on opening to bevies of squatting adventurers. The recent converts to outdoor sojourning and new generations coming along are always in need of guidance and inspiration, and let's not forget *comforting*.

Should you be a person who—sheerly out of dread of the "complete wilderness experience"—tends to remain longingly planted at the edge of a forest others are hiking, on the bank of a river others are floating, I urge you, instead, to . . . READ ON.

Original Preface

In response to Nature's varied calls, *How to Shit in the Woods* presents a collection of techniques (stumbled upon by myself, usually in a most graceless fashion) to assist the latest generation of backwoods enthusiasts still fumbling with their drawers. Just as important is the intention to answer a different, more desperate cry from Nature in conveying essential and explicit environmental precautions about wilderness toiletries applicable to a variety of seasons, climates, and terrains.

For many millennia our ancestors squatted successfully in the woods. You might think it would follow that everyone would know how by instinct. Nature simply takes its course when a colon is bulging or a bladder bursting. But "its course," I cheerlessly and laboriously discovered, was subject to infinite miserable destinations.

Several seasons of guiding city folks down whitewater rivers both sharpened my squatting skills and assured me I wasn't alone in the klutz department. Frequently, the strife and anxiety experienced in the bushes were more intense than any sweat produced by the downstream roar of a monster, raft-eating rapid. Those summers on rivers led me to a couple of firm conclusions. *One:* Monster rapids inspire a lot of squatting, which in turn supports a wealth of study material for *two*. *Two* (and ultimately one of the subjects that prompted this publication): Finesse at shitting in the woods—or anywhere else, for that matter—is not come by instinctively. That might sound as though I were a regular Peeping Joan. But with several dozen bodies squatting behind the few bushes and boulders of a narrow river canyon, I found it practically impossible not to trip over a few—exhibiting all manner of contorted expressions and positions—every day. Generally, a city-bred adult can expect to be no more successful than a tottering one-year-old in dropping his or her pants to squat. Shitting in the woods is an acquired rather than innate skill, a skill honed only by practice, a skill all but lost to the bulk of the population along with the art of making soap, carding wool, and skinning buffalo.

We are now many generations potty-trained on indoor plumbing and accustomed to our privacy, comfort, and convenience. To a person brought up on the spiffy, silenced, flush toilet hidden away behind the bolted bathroom door, elimination in the backcountry can degenerate rapidly into a frightening physical hazard, an embarrassing mess, or, incredibly, a weeklong attack of avoidance constipation.

A lust for wilderness vacations and exotic treks keeps on exploding out of our metropolitan confines. With the same furor that marked the nineteenth-century westward race to fulfill Manifest Destiny, rat race victims now seek respite in the wilds from twenty-first-century urban madness. Masses of bodies are thundering through forests, scurrying up mountain peaks, flailing down rivers, and, without some attention on our part, leaving a wake of toilet paper and fecal matter Mother Nature cannot fathom. It's not unrealistic to fear that within a few more years the last remaining pristine places could well exhibit conditions equal to the world's worst slums.

Anyone who has come upon a favorite, once-lovely beach or riverbank trashed with litter knows the horror. But greater than the visual impact of rapidly increasing human waste in the woods are the veiled environmental consequences. Tragically, no longer can we drink from even the most remote, crystal clear streams without the possibility of contracting giardiasis, a disease spread through fecal deposits in or about the waterways—a disease unknown in the U.S. wilderness prior to the 1970s.

Once the "authorities" have taken over preservation, it is, to my mind, already too late. Rules and regulations imposed by government agencies (although now absolutely necessary in many areas) are themselves rude incursions into majestically primitive surroundings and antipodal to the freedom wildness represents. Rules, signs, application forms, and their ensuing costs are truly a pain in the ass, brought about not solely by increased numbers of persons, but also by the innocently unaware and the blatantly irresponsible. The willingness to inspire preservation comes most naturally from those who delight in the untrammeled wilds; it is they—we—who have the greatest responsibility for respect, care, and education. And it is we who must learn and teach others how and where to shit in the woods.

Author's Note

A collection of scattered ideas on scraps of yellow lined paper, *How to Shit in the Woods* lay in a drawer while I grappled with a seemingly insurmountable problem: terminology. How was I to refer this *stuff* that is pushed and squirted out of bodies in response to eating and drinking?

Since the days of Adam men have been announcing that they were going off to take a piss, leak, dump, or crap. Although references to the subject do not abound in history, conjecture would have Eve and her female descendants declaring the same until those allegedly delicate of heart, weak-stomached Victorian ladies began fainting at the sound of such language. Daintiness and propriety contracted an allergy to the foregoing diction that is considered odious to this day. Yet someday, I suspect, cultural fashion will dictate another sweeping back-to-basics movement and relieve this parlance, currently deemed macho, of its inelegance.

Loathing most things fashionable and having at one time worked with street kids, I confess that my own language can quite easily become delightfully raw and debased. I salute macho (in this instance) in the interest of directness. Still, I was reluctant to begin by offending most readers, education—not alienation—being the goal in mind. The process by which I resolved this semantic difficulty is worth sharing.

In everyday speech around everyday friends, I admit I'm partial to the words *shit* and *pee*. Running through all the alternatives produced no sound solutions. Studding an entire book with *urination, defecation, elimination,* and *stools* seemed depressingly clinical. The pronunciation alone of the terms *bowel movement* and *BM* seems to emit something foul—from my childhood, I remember them being breathed in whispers. *Bathroom* and *restroom* are euphemisms not applicable in the woods; even *outhouse* and *Porta Potti* do not fit where they do not exist. *Scats, turds, dung, chips, pellets,* and *pies* are useful mainly in zoology and dirty jokes. *Constitutional* seems overly prissy in addition to being misleading, since I never heard of anything but a "morning" constitutional, easily confused with a brisk turn in the fresh air. *John, johnny, head, potty, wee-wee, pee-pee, whizz, Number One* and *Number Two, tinkle, poop, load, poo-poo, doo-doo, ca-ca,* and "going to see a man about a horse"—all a little too indirect or too cutesy.

Next, I tried circumventing the problem by relying on description and avoiding particular terms altogether. But the prose became lengthy and cumbersome; plus, I was certain I'd be accused of not calling a crap a crap. There I was, stuck again, and not another noun in sight.

My mind slowly began wandering back over the tangle of verbiage looking for a new trail, something missed. I remembered my father had always purported to be within his genteel rights in using the word *piss* because Shakespeare had employed it. Father's strategy seemed excellent (though he was technically wrong; it was Jonathan Swift), and over the years my refined (verging on priggish) mother did grow, if reluctantly, to accept this argument. Although she never came to use the word herself, in time the wince that wrinkled up her face upon its utterance became almost indiscernible. Thus, with a solid case in point and Mother's brief but significant evolution in mind, a defensible logic began to take hold.

The printed word has a way of inventing truths (as the success of several sleazy national tabloids attests) and of influencing acceptable usage, with *Webster's* dictionary being considered the most reliable reference. A great excitement seized me as I noted that although my 1957 unabridged edition of *Webster's* contained no mention of *shit*, the library's 1988 edition did include the term plus a three-line definition. Aha! What do you know? Linguistic history in the making.

Next, I remembered something E. B. White had written about language that had stuck in my mind, no doubt, because of his choice of metaphor—rivers being close to my heart:

> *The language is perpetually in flux: It is a living stream, shifting, changing, receiving new strength from a thousand tributaries, losing old forms in the backwaters of time.*

Shit hadn't been lost in any backwater. White might well be horrified by my using his explanation for my justifications, but, unwittingly and to my great joy, I found he supplied more and more defense for my crystallizing rationale:

> *A new word is always up for survival. Many do survive. Others grow stale and disappear. Most are, at least in their infancy, more appropriate to conversation than to composition.*

By no means had *shit* grown stale. For hundreds of years *shit* had survived with ease. I knew it to be an old word: I'd seen it written as *scitian* in Old English and as *shyte* in Middle English. Currently, *shit* abounds in daily conversation. But with *Webster's* proclaiming its usage as "vulgar," I concluded the word was lolling in its infancy.

With the needed precedent set in 1988, I fell right into keeping with Father's old strategy. My lacking the literary stature of Shakespeare or Jonathan Swift became no matter. Feeling as exuberant as one of E. B. White's thousand burbling tributaries, I proposed to help wash this great word, *shit*, downstream to its confluence with greater maturity and on into the ocean of acceptable usage. There it might float around in the company of all other words deemed proper for composition. And so it was that I comfortably settled on the promotion of *shit* (and *pee* along with it) accompanied by splashes of clinical and cutesy in appropriate places.

Shit is a superb word, really. Sometimes *shit* can be music to my ears. It doesn't have to be spoken in hushed, moralizing tones. SHIT! OH, SHEEIT! A versatile, articulate, and colorful word, it is indeed a pleasure to shout, to roll along one's tongue. A perfectly audible—if not ear-shattering—remarkably ordinary, decent, modest everyday word.

Furthermore, it was my thought that in legitimately defining *shit*, I might engender some small credibility for the word with anyone still shocked by its usage. *Pee* seems unnecessary to define here, as according to the *Oxford English Dictionary* it is already a euphemism for *piss*. It is also a familiar and cultured sound: we have Ps and peas and appease.

For the too well bred then and the overly delicate, for the betterment of the English language, and perhaps for the next edition of *Webster's*, I offer (it is for the reader to decide whether shamelessly) at the end of the text a complete, unabridged definition of *shit*. For all its subtleties of meaning, this word is extremely unambiguous. *Shit*, in fact, is one of the least misunderstood words in use today.

When I was winding up the second edition of *How to Shit in the Woods*, it occurred to me it might be some few centuries before the word *shit* lost its firecracker appeal to children. I related the following story:

> *Once upon a time, a woman named Tia, a farrier by profession, sat on her commode reading a few pages of the first edition of this book—in fact, the very pages preceding this one. In rolling over in her mind my theories on the evolution of the word shit, she came upon the notion of imparting to her children a new attitude toward the sound of s-h-i-t. Their generation might then, she thought, grow up in plain acceptance of the word, reacting to it as they might now to "puppy" or "bubble gum." At that moment, her seven-year-old son appeared at the bathroom door asking if she would accompany him to the trampoline. On impulse she said, "Just as soon as Mama's through shitting."*
>
> *SHITTING? MAMA'S SHITTING? His eyes bulged, growing round as his trampoline. Out to the yard he ran, broadcasting to his brother and inadvertently the whole neighborhood: "MAMA'S SHITTING!!!"*

It's quite possible that we could coordinate my farrier friend's effort at advancing etymology by synchronizing a time around the globe to tell all seven-year-olds about shitting. Then we can all stand aghast together while our offspring shout to the neighbors. The whole thing should be over in a week.

1 Anatomy of a Crap

Bowels are not exactly a polite subject for conversation, but they are certainly a common problem. . . . Please think of me again as the urologist's daughter. . . . It may disgust you that I have brought it up at all, but who knows? Life has some problems which are basic for all of us—and about which we have a natural reticence.

—Katherine Hepburn, *The Making of The African Queen*

In the mid-1800s, in the Royal Borough of Chelsea, London, an industrious young English plumber named Thomas Crapper grabbed Progress in his pipe wrench and with a number of sophisticated sanitation inventions leapfrogged ahead one hundred years. T. J. Crapper found himself challenged by problems we wrestle with yet today: water quality and water conservation. Faced with London's diminishing reservoirs, drained almost dry by the valve leakage and "continuous flush systems" of early water closets, Crapper developed the *water waste preventer*—the very siphonic cistern with uphill flow and automatic shut-off found in modern toilet tanks. T. Crapper & Co Ld, Sanitary Engineers, Marlboro Works, Chelsea (as his name still appears on three manhole covers in Westminster Abbey) was also responsible for the laying of hundreds of miles of London's connecting sewers—and none too soon. The River Thames carried such quantities of rotting turds that the effluvium had driven Parliament to convene in the early morning hours to avoid a vile off-river breeze.

For the Victorian ladies who complained of the WC's hissing and gurgling as giving away their elaborately disguised trips to the loo, Crapper installed the first silencers. Such pretenses as "pricking the plum pudding" or "picking the daisies" were foiled when a lady's absence was accompanied by crashing waterfalls and echoing burbles. Among Mr. Crapper's other claims to fame were his pear-shaped toilet seat (the forerunner of the gap-front seat) designed for men, and the posthumous addition to the English language of a vibrant new word: *crapper*!

Clearly, T. J. Crapper was ahead of his day. Progress and time, nonetheless, are peculiar concepts. Some things in the universe—pollution, the use of euphemisms, *sneaking* off to the bathroom to tinkle silently down the side of the bowl, to name a few—seem to defy change, even from century to century. But there's been one glaring reversal in regard to crap. Our advanced twenty-first-century populace, well removed from the novelties and quirks of the first indoor WCs, finds itself having to break entirely new ground, as it were, when relieving itself outdoors. Ironically, shitting in the woods successfully—that is, without adverse environmental, psychological, or physical consequences—might be deemed genuine progress today. Take Henry, for instance (a namesake, perhaps, or even a descendant of old King Henry VIII).

All the stories you are about to read are true (for the most part), having been extracted from dear friends and voluble strangers on various occasions, sometimes following the ingestion of copious quantities of Jose Cuervo or Yukon Jack. Only the names have been changed to protect the incommodious.

High on a dusty escarpment jutting skyward from camp, a man named Henry, having scrambled up there and squeezed in behind what appeared to be the ideal bush for camouflage, began lowering himself precariously into a deep knee bend. Far below, just out of their bedrolls, three fellow river runners violated the profound quiet of the canyon's first light by poking about the commissary, cracking eggs, snapping twigs, and sloshing out the coffee pot. Through the branches, our pretzel man on the hill observed the breakfast preparations while proceeding with his own morning mission. To the earth it finally fell, round and firm, this sturdy turd. With a bit more encouragement from gravity, it rolled slowly out from between Henry's big boots, threaded its way through the spindly trunks of the "ideal" bush, and then truly taking on a mind of its own, leaped into the air like a down-hill skier out at the gate.

You can see the dust trail of a fast-moving pickup mushrooming off a dirt road long after you've lost sight of the truck. Henry watched, wide-eyed and helpless, as a similar if smaller cloud billowed up defiantly below him, and the actual item became obscured from view. Zigging and zagging, it caromed off rough spots in the terrain. Madly it bumped and tumbled and dropped, as though making its run through a giant pinball machine. Gaining momentum, gathering its own little avalanche, round and down it spun like a buried back tire spraying up sand. All too fast it raced down the steep slope—until it became locked into that deadly slow motion common to the fleeting seconds just preceding all imminent, unalterable disasters. With one last bounce, one final effort at heavenward orbit, this unruly goof ball (followed by an arcing tail of debris) landed in a terminal thud and a rain of pebbly clatter not six inches from the bare foot of the woman measuring out coffee.

With his dignity thus unraveled along sixty yards of descent, Henry in all likelihood might have come home from his first river trip firmly resolved to never again set foot past the end of the asphalt. Of course, left to his own devices and with any determination at all unless he was a total fumble-bum, Henry would have learned how to shit in the woods. Eventually. The refining of his skills by trial and error and the acquiring of grace, poise, and self-confidence—not to mention muscle development and balance— would probably have taken him about as long as it did me: years.

I don't think Henry would mind our taking a closer look at his calamity. Henry can teach us a lot, and not all by poor example. Indeed, he started out on the right track by getting far enough away from camp to ensure his privacy. Straight up just wasn't the best choice of direction. Next, he chose a location with a view, although whether he took time to appreciate it is unknown. Usually I recommend a wide-reaching view, a landscape rolling away to distant mountain peaks and broad expanses of wild sky. But a close-in setting near a lichen-covered rock, a single wildflower, or even dried-up weeds and monotonous talus, when quietly studied, can offer inspiration of a different brand.

The more time you spend in the wild, the easier it will be to reconnoiter an inspiring view. A friend of mine calls her morning exercise the Advanced Wilderness Appreciation Walk. As she strides along an irrigation canal practically devoid of vegetation, but overgrown with crumpled beer cans, has-been appliances, and rusted auto parts, she finds the morning's joy in the colors of the sunrise and the backlighting of a lone thistle.

Essential for the outdoor neophyte is a breathtaking view. These opportunities for glorious moments alone in the presence of grandeur should be soaked up. They are soul replenishing and mind expanding. The ideal occasion for communing with nature is while you're peacefully sitting still—yes, shitting in the woods. The rest of the day, unless you're trekking solo, can quickly become cluttered with social or organizational distractions.

But back to Henry, whose only major mistake was failing to dig a hole. It's something to think about: a small hole preventing the complete destruction of an ego. A proper hole is of great importance, not only in averting disasters such as Henry's, but in preventing the spread of disease and facilitating rapid decomposition. Chapter 2 in its entirety is devoted to *the hole*.

More do's and don'ts for preserving mental and physical health while shitting in the woods will become apparent as we look in on Charles. He has his own notion about clothes and pooping in the wilderness: he takes them off. Needless to say, this man hikes well away from camp and any connecting trails to a place where he feels secure about completely removing his britches and relaxing for a spell. Finding an ant-free log, he digs his hole on the opposite side from the view, sits down, scoots to the back of the log, and floats into the rhapsody that tall treetops find in the clouds. Remember this one. It's by far the dreamiest, most relaxing setup for shitting in the woods. A smooth, breadloaf-shaped rock (or even your backpack in a pinch in a vacant wasteland) can be used in the same manner—for hanging your buns over the back.

This seems like an appropriate spot to share a helpful technique imparted to me one day by another friend: "Shit first, dig later." In puzzlement, I turned to her and as our eyes met she watched mine grow into harvest moons. But of course, "shit first, dig later"—that way you could never miss the hole. It was the perfect solution! Perfect, that is, for anyone with bad aim. Me? Not me.

Unlike Charles, there's my longtime friend Elizabeth who prizes the usefulness of her clothes. While on a rattletrap bus trip through northern Mexico, the lumbering vehicle on which she rode came to a five-minute halt to compensate for the lack of a toilet on board. Like a colorful parachute descending from desert skies, Lizzie's voluminous skirt billowed to the earth, and she squatted down inside her own private outhouse.

Occasionally it is impossible to obtain an optimal degree of privacy. Some years back, my colleague Henrietta Alice was hitchhiking along the Autobahn in Germany, where the terrain was board flat and barren. At last, unable to contain herself, she asked the driver to stop and she struck out across a field toward a knoll topped by a lone bush. There, hidden by branches and feeling safe from the eyes of traffic, she squatted and swung up the back of her skirt, securing it as a cape over her head. But Henrietta's rejoicing ended abruptly. Out of nowhere came a column of Boy Guides (the rear guard?) marching past her bare derrière.

Another version of Henrietta's story needs to be kept in mind when hiking switchbacks. I was all settled once, well off the path, completely shrouded with low-hanging branches, pants down, a soft mullein leaf in hand, when smack at me came three hikers, all men, stepping smartly along on the previous bend in the trail. Only the footway's ruts and roots, which held their attention, and my holding my breath like a startled squirrel saved me.

There are many theories on clothes and shitting, all individual and personal. In time you will develop your own. Edwin, our next case study, has a new theory about clothes after one memorable hunting trip; whether it be to take them off or keep them on, I haven't figured out.

For the better part of a nippy fall morning, Edwin had been slinking through whole mountain ranges of gnarly underbrush in pursuit of an elusive six-pointer. Relentlessly trudging along with no luck, he finally became discouraged; a cold drizzle added to his gloom. Then a lovely meadow opened before him, its beauty causing him to pause. His attention averted from the deer, he now relaxed into a gaze of pleasure, and soon became aware of his physical discomforts: every weary muscle, every labored joint, every miniscule bramble scratch—and then another pressing matter.

Coming upon a log beneath a spreading tree, Edwin propped up his rifle, quickly slipped off his poncho, and slid the suspenders from his shoulders. Whistling now, he sat and he shat. But when he turned to bid it farewell, not a thing was there *there*. Oh, hell! In total disbelief, Edwin peered over the log once more, still finding nothing. The sky opened and it began to rain and a pleasant vision of camp beckoned. Preparing to leave, he yanked on his poncho and hefted his gun. To warm his ears, he pulled up his hood. There it was! On top of his head, melting in the rain like a scoop of ice cream left in the sun.

Poor Edwin will not soon forget this day; he walked seven miles before coming across enough water to get cleaned up. Though I fear he was in no humor to be thinking much beyond himself, we can only hope he didn't wash directly in the stream. To keep pollutants from entering the waterways, it's important to use a bucket to haul wash water well above the high-water line of spring runoff. But I digress, and this topic is covered thoroughly in the next chapter. For now, back to techniques.

When he was eighty-six years old, my dear Uncle Ernie was cautioning old people fearful of toppling over while squatting (old people?) to steady themselves by holding on to a branch or tree trunk. It's lately come to my attention that Uncle Ernie's tactic requires an added warning. Sergio Jaurequi, longtime Baja guide and owner of Todo Santos Eco Travel, related an episode collected from one of his hiking clients. We'll call her Susie Falls Down Squish. Sergio came by this rather personal story because Susie, after announcing she'd be "right back," apparently felt the need to explain her great tardiness in returning to camp. She had trotted off originally on a mission of evacuation. While in a squat, she'd sought to steady herself by grabbing on to a branch. The branch snapped! "What might have taken her ten minutes," Sergio said, with a sympathetic wince, "stretched into an hour." Hence, should Uncle Ernie's approach be one that appeals to you, be sure to select a strong and living branch on a species that is not brittle—or, you, like Susie, could land precisely in the spot that you rather would not. My theory is to find a place to sit: I'm really Charles, the sitting dreamer, in disguise.

If you're a good squatter and also in a hurry, perhaps to chase a caribou or click off pictures of the sunset, you might try a technique perfected by one of our elected U.S. officials. We'll call him Jonathan the Deer Hunter, and, I might add, the Ham. His is a rare performance, an adagio of fluid motion and perfect balance. One night after midnight, at the tail end of a venison barbecue bash, I mentioned I was writing this book and received a narrated mock demonstration on the living room rug.

Sinking into a hang ten surfboard pose—knees bent and arms outstretched from the shoulders—Jonathan scrapes a trench four to five inches deep with the heel of one cowboy boot. "This works," he says, "only where the earth is soft." Addressing those of us still left in the living room, he suggests dropping your jeans (and drops his) either to just below your hips or all the way to your ankles, pointing out that folds of material are uncomfortable when bunched up in the bends at the back of your knees. After squat-straddling the ditch for as long as it takes, he drops in his paper and shoves the excavated dirt back into the trough with the instep of his boot. As a finale, he packs down the dirt the way any good gardener would finish planting a tree. It was a marvelous performance, I had to agree, except for the toilet paper in the hole—the telltale sign of humans on the planet. We'll discuss this later.

From the depths of many a lumpy sleeping bag, from the middle of many a wilderness campsite, has come this sort of question accompanied by a bit of a whine: "Herbert? Whaddo I do if I have to go in the middle of the night?" Secretly, Herbert might harbor an identical first-time question, so I'll answer this one for him.

Unless there's a full moon or you have the nocturnal instincts of the snails that go for my petunias, carry a flashlight for those midnight jaunts. As much as I dislike anything resembling civilization in the boondocks, I will concede that in unfamiliar terrain, a tiny lightbulb can prevent a stubbed toe, a cracked head—when you trip and pitch over the cliff—or, more commonly, two weeks of itchy crotch-crazies from lurking poison oak. Many contributors to this book have confessed to one of those "I hoped I wouldn't live long enough to tell the story" stories. Poison oak (or ivy or sumac) seems to be the most common misadventure of night squatting.

One further warning: make it a *small* flashlight. The searchlight variety is overkill and can predispose the body to more permanent damage from irate fellow campers. There's nothing like waking up in the middle of peaceful nowhere to someone crashing through the bushes with her high beams and a roll of toilet paper.

Observant caution is always the recommended approach in selecting a place to relieve oneself. Poison oak is not the only dastardly culprit abroad. As my friend Ma Prudence Barker notes, one cannot just plop down with wild abandon in any old daisy field— especially a daisy field—and hope to escape unscathed. Ma once knew a logger named Lloyd who experienced the unequivocal misery of being nailed by a bumblebee smack on the family jewels. Logger Lloyd swore the pain was worse than any chainsaw nick, bullet hole, or careless imprint of Currins Caulk tearing into flesh.

It is prudent to inspect any area for hazards where you plan to sit down bare-assed. You wouldn't want to become an outdoor casualty, as did the subject of this poem by Shirley Vogler Meister.

> **The Ex-Camper**
> *Though city-bred, he learned to camp*
> *and loved to trek in dew and damp*
> *until a creeping critter found*
> *him crouching with his denims down.*

My own stinging affair transpired on a late-afternoon saunter along the ever-captivating Bitterroot River, near my home. Half a mile downstream from the fishing access, I began to hear nature's call, and it grew rapidly into a booming holler. "You can always skip a meal," a friend once said, "but when you gotta go, you gotta go!" I beelined across the cobblestone beach, up the embankment, and into the woodlands. Immediately—and fortuitously, I thought at the time—I came upon an area of deadfall that presented several downed trees and quickly selected a handy one, smooth-trunked and requiring only the tossing aside of an overlying branch. I was unbuttoning my cargo pants and stripping down the straps of my one-piece bathing suit when a buzzing that didn't register as threatening trained my eyes to a slab of bark canted over the grasses at my feet. *Oh, yuck! Someone's been here and done their doody!* I was envisioning a pack of intently busy flies, when zow-wee! Nailed! On the shoulder, the underarm, the back. Wildly swiping at the attack, I ran, stumbling, screaming back to the beach. Ground-nesting yellow jackets are among the fiercest of hornets. In retrospect, I can't believe I didn't spontaneously load up my pants. The urge, in fact, completely shut down until my strolling partner had removed fourteen stingers from welts the size of fifty-cent-pieces and I was again home.

Is there a moral to this story? Well, for me, there is: keep on teaching outdoor toilet etiquette, in order to better trust that other river walkers won't be leaving messy piles under hunks of bark. And then, at first sign of buzzing, RUN LIKE CRAZY.

Stay alert for the presence of other critters. Snakes are notorious for snoozing tucked under rocks and logs. Ants run around everywhere. And there are places in the world, as the noted writer and explorer Tim Cahill discovered, where a person can't squat (to shit) without carrying a big stick to beat off the local pigs. Always check around for damage you might incur, and check for damage you might inflict.

One morning on the Owyhee River in Oregon, our party had already broken camp, loaded the boats, and tied down everything securely. We were standing ready to push off into the current when it became apparent to me that the morning's coffee had arrived at the end of its course through my innards.

"Wait, wait," I cried to everyone and raced up the bank, winding through the jumble of boulders until a convenient rock presented itself. Yanking down my shorts, I sat down and began to water the face of the rock.

Now the southeastern corner of Oregon is home to the chukar, a relative of the partridge. This chunky, chickenlike bird is saddled with a reputation for being absurdly stupid and has the added hereditary misfortune of a lunatic voice. A cuckoo bird with the hiccups couldn't sound sillier. Audubon calls the chukar a "hardy game bird that can outrun a hunter (first flying uphill, then flying down)." It's been my experience that if you decided upon a chukar for dinner, you could walk right up to one, hand it a stone, and it would agreeably hit itself over the head for you. Combine the bird's inability for anything resembling graceful flight with its darting, quickstepping motion reminiscent of an old-time movie, add long hours spent ridiculously burping its own name, and the chukar becomes cause for much amusement.

Still propped on the rock, I was appreciating a final glance around one of my favorite river camps while enjoying the pleasure of a shrinking bladder. Suddenly, there came a loud, crazed *chukkarr chuk-karr*. A great flapping motion arose from between my knees, convulsed into my face, and then vanished. I knelt down before the wet rock. Tucked beneath a small overhang, behind a clump of grass, I found a precious woven nest holding eight warm eggs—now lakefront property on the edge of a puddle of piss. In one great swoop of karma, all my abusive snickering and pompous guffawing, my enjoyment at the expense of this poor species of fowl, had come home to roost and I felt terrible. Atop a nearby boulder after her fit of apoplexy, the ruffled mother sat staring at me. While heading back to the beach, I chided the powers that be for not giving me a more acute sense of smell or hearing—in the absence of experience—and resolved to do more vigorous battle with my ignorance.

Most of the foregoing stories are worst-case scenarios. I have recounted them not to scare you out of the woods, but to acknowledge real perils and suggest how to work around them. Life itself is a risk; you could trip headlong over your own big toe or swallow your breakfast down the wrong pipe any day of the week. And have you ever tried to locate a toilet downtown—a task fraught with more frustration than any possible misfortune outdoors? Someone (not me) really needs to produce a handbook on how to shit in the city.

I'll just say this: disasters of elimination in the city can be more excruciatingly humiliating than those in the bush. Sometimes I think storekeepers and clerks all must be terribly regular, "going" at home in the morning and then not needing a *terlit* (as my grandmother from Brooklyn would have said) for the rest of the day. If there is a grime-coated john tucked away in the far reaches of a musty storeroom, for some reason this information is as heavily guarded as the most clandestine revolutionary plans. In tramping around town, I've all too often encountered locked doors, scribbled *Out of Order* signs, *Employees Only* plaques, or "I'm sorry we don't have one" fibs. Sometimes the only recourse is to streak for home and hope to arrive in time. Me, I'll take the backcountry.

So, get on out there. Find a place of privacy, a "place of easement" as the Elizabethans knew it. Find a panoramic view—one that can't be had with the twist of the handle on a steel cubicle. Go for it!

2 Digging the Hole

Landscape is sacramental, to be read as text.
—Seamus Heaney, *Preoccupations*

When we try to pick something by itself, we find it hitched to everything else in the universe.
—John Muir, *Daily Journal*, 1869

Now for the serious stuff. People—Wall Street barons, corporate CEOs, philandering spouses, presidential candidates—always want to know how to bury their shit. This chapter spells out precisely where and how to dig holes that promote rapid decomposition of feces and prevent contamination of waterways, thereby providing the best protection for the health of humans, the remainder of the animal kingdom, and the planet. Before we can hope to fathom how great is the importance of properly digging our own small *one-sit* hole (also termed a *cat hole*) in the bush, it's necessary to try to envision our shit in the global sense. *Try* is the trick here.

Exactly where does the world's collective excrement go? Not a pleasant question. How often do any of us ponder where it goes after it's sucked down the hole in the bottom of the bowl? Possibly never. Such reflections tend to detour our consciousness, barring those rare occasions when we have to call Roto-Rooter.

Approached from any angle, the actual physical dimensions of this pile of crap produced upon our globe befuddle imagining.

Nevertheless, let's go back to the Mesozoic era and try thinking across the ages—across mountain ranges, across continents—to the present. Let's begin with dinosaur scats.

In all probability, the *Stegosaurus* and *Tyrannosaurus rex* let rip with something the size of a HUMMER. The piles left by the woolly tusked mammoth might have been somewhat smaller, say, Mini Cooper–sized—nonetheless, a formidable turd. To the total of the dinosaurs' leavings add the excrement of Cro-Magnon man (and woman) and the wandering tribes. Add the feces of polar bears, black bears, brown bears, gorillas, hippos, and giraffes. Add buffalo chips. Add tiger and rhino dung. Tally up the dumps of the Romans (remembering their gluttonous ways), the Vikings (that stout-of-digestion breed), and modern man, woman, and infant (by all means, infant—we know how the human baby goes at it). Include the scats of elephant and lion, deer and antelope, moose and kangaroo, caribou and wallaby. Toss in every species that birdshits—from pterodactyl to parakeet. Round up the output of hogs, dogs, horses, cows, rabbits, owls, cats, and rats. And in imagining all this, you'll have put a mere chicken scratch on the surface.

Anyone who's been responsible for the maintenance of a cat's litter box understands how turds have an inherent tendency to pile up like junk mail. And anyone who has skipped across a cow pasture has spent at least a few seconds marveling at the size of those rippled pies (if not sailing the dried ones like Frisbees). Now, multiply one—just one—litter box or cow by 230 million years. Gadzooks!

Since the minutest scrap of life began wriggling around on our planet, Mother Earth has valiantly been embracing fecal waste in an astounding display of her natural absorption capacities. An infinitely bottomless garbage pit, however, does not exist. There are times when the amount of waste becomes far too great for it to be amassed comfortably against her bosom. And the amount of the waste can often have less to do with the problem than the manner in which it's discarded.

Take, for instance, all the campers in a national park on one good-weather weekend and imagine them as a herd of buffalo corralled in a space the size of your backyard. Or take a boatload of refugees, rolling and tossing, seasick on ocean swells, and visualize them locked (but fed) for two months inside your favorite movie theater, without plumbing. In the absence of properly functioning or adequately dug disposal facilities, accumulated fecal matter rapidly grows into a major sanitation problem, sometimes with devastating consequences. Under such conditions, diseases find king-size footholds from which to run rampant. Epidemics— not to mention assaults on the aesthetics—are common in regions where the tonnage of yuck exceeds absorption capacities. Fecally transmitted diseases are endemic in most developing countries, but they are not unheard of in the United States.

Until roughly the mid-1970s, no one ever considered it unsafe to drink directly from mountain streams. You could stretch out on the bank of a high mountain meadow creek and just push your face into the water to drink. In 1977, the Sierra Club backpacker's guide still touted drinking directly from wilderness waterways as one of the "very special pleasures" of backcountry travel. In 1968, Edward Abbey wrote the following in *Desert Solitaire*, (New York: Ballantine, 1985):

> *When late in the afternoon I finally stumbled—sun-dazed, blear-eyed, parched as an old bacon rind—upon that blue stream which flows like a miraculous mirage down the floor of the canyon, I was too exhausted to pause and drink soberly from the bank. Dreamily, deliriously, I waded into the waist-deep water and fell on my face. Like a sponge I soaked up moisture through every pore, letting the current bear me along beneath a canopy of overhanging willow trees. I had no fear of drowning in the water—I intended to drink it all.*

But no longer can we *drink it all*—no longer can we drink even a drop before purifying it without running the risk of getting sick. According to the Centers for Disease Control and Prevention (CDC) in Atlanta, no surface water in the world is guaranteed free of the microscopic cysts responsible for a parasitic disease called giardiasis. This is a disease not easily eradicated, either in the wilds or in the human body. Although not fatal in healthy adults, it can be an unpleasant and debilitating illness and, in some cases, chronic. For the very young, the old, or the frail, it can be worse. It is also possible to have the disease, show no symptoms, but, nonetheless, be a carrier. In the medical community in some locations, giardiasis is still an obscure disease and the general public can be instrumental in promoting an awareness of it. To that end, I've reprinted here a list of specific symptoms.

Symptoms of Giardiasis (commonly called *Giardia*)

1. Sudden onset of explosive diarrhea seven to ten days after ingestion, especially in conjunction with wilderness or foreign travel (other sources to consider are dogs, cats, and preschool daycare centers).
2. A large volume of foul-smelling, loose (but not watery) stools, accompanied by abdominal distention, flatulence, and cramping.
3. Nausea, vomiting, lack of appetite, headache, and low-grade fever.
4. Acute symptoms can last seven to twenty-one days, and can become chronically persistent or relapsing.
5. In chronic cases, significant weight loss can occur due to malabsorption.
6. In chronic cases, bulky, loose, foul-smelling stools—or greasy, light-colored stools that tend to float—can persist or recur.
7. Chronic symptoms include flatulence, bloating, constipation, and upper abdominal cramps.

(Although it's thought that most cases resolve spontaneously within four to six weeks, if you think you have *Giardia*, you should see your health care provider for stool testing and medication. With any diarrhea illness, replenishing body fluids is critical. Keep in mind that the symptoms given above are nonspecific; many other problems can exhibit the same symptoms. In fact, when testing stool samples nowadays, it is recommended to test for both *Giardia* and another protozoan prolific in surface waters, *Cryptosporidium*, discussed later in this chapter.)

The actual spread of the *Giardia lamblia* parasite into the back-country is an interesting and as yet incomplete story. Although the particulars of transmission are still under study, it has been determined that strains can be passed between animals and humans. Like many of the world's enteric pathogens (intestinal bugs), *Giardia* is spread by "fecal-oral" transmission, meaning some form of the infectious organism is shed in feces and enters a new host or victim by way of the mouth. The *Giardia lamblia* protozoan has a two-stage life cycle. The active stage, the tropho-zoite, feeds and reproduces in the intestine of the animal host; any *live* trophozoites excreted in feces die off rapidly. The second stage, the dormant cyst, which is also passed in fecal matter, is much hardier and able to survive in an outside environment.

Direct fecal-oral transmission of *Giardia* cysts is a concern in preschool daycare centers and other institutions. This type of transmission by direct person-to-person contact (and via contam-inated food) can easily be eliminated in town or the outback with careful attention to washing hands. It is the waterborne transmis-sion that poses a bigger problem in the wilds. Once the cysts have entered lakes and streams, they can remain viable for months—particularly in cold waters.

Giardia cysts have been discovered in mountain headwaters, the alpine feeders that spring to life from rainfall and eventu-ally wash down to form all our watercourses. Concentrations are higher in some rivers and streams than in others; studies show that both occurrence and concentrations change region-ally and seasonally. It is still very possible to scoop a cupful of pure water directly from a stream, but the risks aren't worth it. Technically, as soon as water falls from the sky and lands on the ground or bubbles to the surface from a natural spring, it is pos-sible for *Giardia* to be present. Only a few cysts need be ingested and enter our intestinal track to cause infection. In "Eat, Drink, and Be Wary" (reprinted from California Wilderness Coalition in *Headwaters*, Friends of the River, March/April 1984), Thomas

Suk discusses various paths by which fecal material enters wilderness waterways:

> . . . *direct deposition by humans or animals into water, and deposition near water where the cysts can be carried into the water by runoff, rising water levels, erosion, or on the feet of humans and animals. Cysts may also be carried to water on the haircoat of animals who roll in feces.*

Giardia is present nowadays in much of the animal kingdom, with strains having been found in fish, birds, reptiles, and many mammalian species. Animal feces continue to contaminate remote watersheds, although it is not completely clear just how many are transferable to humans (or vice versa). Beavers and muskrats, who spend their lives in the water, are known carriers. But the saddest commentary on the disease is that humans might play a substantial role in spreading it around the world.

Prior to 1970, there were no reports in the United States of waterborne outbreaks of *Giardia*. The first came out of Aspen, Colorado, in 1970. Over the next four years, many cases of *Giardia* were documented in travelers returning from, of all places, Leningrad. The explanation for this was twofold: the Soviet Union had become more open to visitation by Westerners about that time and Leningrad's municipal water supply was full of *Giardia* cysts. The U.S. outbreak sparked debate and speculation, as well as ongoing research, into *Giardia*'s origins and the manner of transmission among species. Where did it come from? Who gave it to whom? Who bears the greatest responsibility for its spread: animals or humans? What do we do now?

A popular theory, seeming to exonerate humans, is that *Giardia* has been around all along—throughout the eons—and is only now being correctly diagnosed. "Around" could be the key word in this theory. *Giardia* might well have been around somewhere, but in the Sierras? In the Rockies? Undeniably, in other parts of the world there have been reports of *Giardia* since it was discovered in 1681. I can't help but recall that numerous river cronies and I drank from watersheds all over the western U.S. and Canada throughout the late 1960s and into the mid-1970s and never came down with *Giardia*—other intestinal disorders on occasion, but not *Giardia*. Only in the late seventies and early eighties did we begin to hear repeatedly of unshakable cases of this "new disease" among us. It seems improbable that we were all previously either asymptomatic carriers or misdiagnosed.

To further humor my personal suspicions as to where the responsibility for the spread of *Giardia* lies, I offer a few more thoughts. If left *solely* to the animals in the wild, it seems the progression might have marched along at a different pace, beaver to beaver, stretching over a long period of time—hundreds, even thousands of years (perhaps never to have reached us at all owing to Darwinian selection or a buildup of natural immunities). It is known that both humans and animals can and do spread this disease. There is also evidence to suggest that animals can rid themselves of *Giardia* during the winter months only to be reinfected by humans in the spring.

For a long time, New Zealand's wilderness waterways, for reasons not altogether clear, were reported *Giardia*-free—possibly because of the country's strict quarantine regulations on all incoming livestock and pets, the island's inherent isolation, and/or the absence of indigenous water mammals. In 1991, we sadly learned that *Giardia* had reached New Zealand's pristine shores. The following year, at opposite ends of the earth, another *Giardia*-free pocket succumbed: Nahanni National Park, a remote area (access by fly-in only) in Canada's Northwest Territories.

Another parasite, with the impressive name *Cryptosporidium* (causing the illness cryptosporidiosis), is also found in backcountry surface waters and sometimes with more frequency and in higher concentrations than *Giardia*. *Cryptosporidium* may sound familiar to you; it made headlines in 1993, as the cause of a waterborne outbreak in Milwaukee that affected in the neighborhood of 400,000 people. As a protozoan, it is similar to *Giardia* in all the following ways: fecal-oral transmission, intestinal propagation, viability in water for long periods, passage between humans and animals, characteristics of acute symptoms, potential for chronic affliction, and occurrence of asymptomatic carriers. *Cryptosporidium*, however, is highly resistant to chlorine (much more so than *Giardia* is). The estimated twenty-one million Americans who receive municipal drinking water from systems dependent on chlorination without filtration are at risk. In other words: don't stay home merely in the hope of avoiding contaminated drinking water. For backcountry travelers, there are many field water filtration systems that will eliminate protozoan parasites.

Before drinking, here is what you must do: treat all backcountry surface water—stream, lake, waterfall. Treat springwater unless it's contained in a concrete housing that provides security against contamination from surface water and animal feces. Keep in mind that the water is only as good as the housing; springs with old crumbling or cracked housings are suspect. Finally, treat even municipal drinking water in developing countries and also when advised in the U.S. For backcountry treatment systems and advice, see chapter 5.

Now for the roaring debate about *Giardia*. Several times in recent years it's come to my attention that there are quite a number of wilderness trekkers pooh-poohing the notion of widespread *Giardia*. These hikers swear by NOT carrying field water treatment apparatus. Having to filter water all along the way of an extended hike is, I'll agree, time-consuming and a wholly irksome task when wanting to get back to the simplicities of Nature. Surely Jane and Tarzan never interrupted their jungle communing to thump away on a pump. Yet starting a debate with a personal account of not contracting *Giardia*—in, say, a lifetime of tramping the backcountry—and expanding it to mean broader evidence that no one is at risk, is risky in itself. Theories of this kind are often stated with bald adamancy. I also hear less vociferously delivered opinions coming from cherished friends, one of whom has taken to skimming lake water off the surface, with the idea that *Giardia* cysts sink; another drinks water straight from a stream in seasons of low water, but not during spring runoff when he envisions *everything* washing into waterways; and a third quenches her thirst directly from creeks close to headwaters, but not downstream. The latter two ideas have some seeming, but not proven, merit. As for skimming lakes—lake water constantly circulates. If we could remove cysts by allowing water to settle, we'd already be doing it.

Before weighing in any further on this subject, let me state that I hold no stock or options in field water treatment companies and receive no free samples. When in need of equipment, I trot down to my local outdoor store and purchase items outright. Now, commencing with those folks who will even profess to having brought back samples of wilderness water and taken them in for testing: don't believe them! Or, at least, press for further details. For such an undertaking, one has to be not only a bodybuilder but also wealthy. Although stool specimens can be tested quite easily and inexpensively in numerous lab facilities, when it comes to actual wilderness water, a fifteen-liter sample (that's more than a half-full 5-gallon bucket) is required for the analysis—imagine someone's lugging that out of the high country, just to prove a point.

But hold on, that's not all. Then you fork over $400. Yes, per test. But say you did this, that you got this far and the test came back negative and you're set to run out and crow around town what you've discovered. What have you really discovered? Simply that *Giardia* cysts were not floating past that certain spot during the moments your were collecting your sample. When the CDC says that *Giardia* is present in all the world's surface water, they don't mean in every cupful. Remember? It's rather a game of Russian roulette. Yet there are those people, I swear, who have an inordinately powerful Lady Luck riding around in their intestines.

Which leads me to mentioning a different batch of stories that have also come to my notice—of those individuals who've been roaming the wilderness for as long as thirty years, drinking freely and never contracting *Giardia*, only finally to find themselves afflicted. I'd be inclined to follow, at minimum, the precautions of Walkin' Jim Stoltz, longtime long-distance hiker, adventurer, writer, musician, and showman (www.walkinjim.com). There was a time, he tells me, when he drank straight from any old source: mud puddles to, accidentally, a stream of toxic waste. Then in the 1980s, in Bryce Canyon, "a nasty bout of gastric ailment," he said, "ruined my walk," although not, to his knowledge, *Giardia*. Since then, he drinks water neat only from carefully scouted sources in the high country and, otherwise, "not wanting to endanger the life of a trip," he carries a small filtration pump.

In the final analysis, in the continuing search to accurately determine the reasons for the spread of *Giardia* and *Cryptosporidium*, one earnest issue comes to light above all others: it is a matter of grave import for us—animals, such as we are, in possession of great mental capacity—to recognize the potential extent of our impact on the total animal kingdom. Too often we fail to take fully into account the ramifications of our fast-living, expedient ways, which reverberate through every other aspect of life on the planet—eventually boomeranging to haunt us. In retrospect, the appearance of these parasites could be of great benefit to us, if they teach us only that we are capable of spreading odd, new diseases as fast as we take vacations. What animal other than *Homo sapiens* can swallow *rogani gosht* in India or *Kalya e Khaas* in South Africa and shit it into the Colorado countryside?

Permit me one last muse on the global subject of spreading diseases before we take up our trowels to dig holes. In most of Africa and parts of the Middle East and South America, surface waters are infested with *Schistosomes*, the blood flukes that cause schistosomiasis (also called Bilharzia after the discovering physician). The presence of these flukes precludes any swimming or wading, as their manner of entry is through the skin. Into these waters, the late great environmental activist Edward Abbey would not have dared dip even his parched big toe to cool off. Fortunately for us in North America, one stage of a *Schistosome*'s life cycle must take place in a snail found only in the tropics. But then again, who out there can promise me that at some future date a minor mutation in the blood fluke's thermostat or, what's more probable, changes in world climate might not leave this parasite completely compatible with our temperate-zone, garden-variety escargot? Unlikely, maybe, but if not Bilharzia, then something else is bound to arrive upon our shores (probably already has).

The best line of defense for protecting our wild lands, our wild friends, and ourselves is to develop scrupulous habits of disposal—dig an environmentally sound hole and bury that shit!—and a compulsion for educating newcomers to the woods with similar fastidiousness.

Now, pick up your backpacker's trowel or old army-entrenching tool and let's go digging.

For those lacking a proper tool, the **U-DIG-IT** ($18 to $20) is a palm-sized stainless steel trowel with a folding handle and a belt sheath. You can plant trees with this instrument and never torque it into the useless half gainer I've made out of numerous cheaper models. It's been tested in military survival schools and is guaranteed not to bend or rust for five years. (**U-DIG-IT** • 3953 Brookside Lane • Boise, ID 83714 • Phone: 208-939-8656 • Email: u-dig-it@msn.com)

Choosing a good excavation site for the one-sit hole requires some knowledge and preparation. The overall objective in burying human fecal matter is to inhibit the passing of disease-causing organisms—by humans, interested animals, or storm runoff—into nearby surface waters, and by flying insects back to food areas.

There is no one best set of rules for all terrains, seasons, and climates. In fact, such a collection of variables and trade-offs exists that at first it might seem one would need four PhDs to sort them all out. For example, the decomposition rate of buried feces is greatly influenced by all of the following: soil type and texture, filterability (as measured in percolation rates), moisture content, slope of terrain, general exposure, insect inhabitation, soil pH, and temperature.

The trade-offs in environmental protection are between security and decomposition. The ideal spot for rapid decomposition (*rapid* is completely relative here; under the best conditions, human shit can take more than a year to vanish) is in soil that's dry to somewhat moist, but not excessively moist, and has abundant humus and bacteria. To better understand this description, think of the perfect place as being shaded part of the day by vegetation that annually sheds its leaves—but not in a drainage area affected by storm runoff or at a site intermittently inundated by an annual rise in water table.

Feces deposited in extremely parched soils in open locations will not be at much risk of removal by runoff. But this kind of ground is difficult to dig into, and the lack of bacterial activity in the meager topsoil could mean that deposits take nigh on forever to decompose. Above timberline and in subzero climates, bacterial activity is virtually nonexistent. In such spots, it is better to pack out your poop—no kidding!—at least back to where it can be buried in good earth, and most often right on back to the trailhead or home. In highly limited conditions there is a further option: *frosting*. Procedures for *packing-it-out* and *frosting* will be covered in chapters 3 and 4.

If you are interested in becoming a burying expert or boggling your mind further with all these variables, Harry Reeves wrote a fascinating article, "Human Waste Disposal in the Sierran Wilderness" (*Wilderness Impact Studies*, San Francisco Sierra Club Outing Committee), reporting the findings of an extensive field study. For the rest of us, one wise philosopher stated it well, "One can do *only* what one can do," and so it is with the search for the ideal hole. Our goal, therefore, will be to dig holes that are as ecologically sound and as aesthetically pleasing as our layman's knowledge and the rest of this chapter will allow.

The primary consideration in choosing a burial site is to prevent feces from becoming washed into any waterway. Even when buried, the bacteria in human waste are capable of traveling a good distance through the surrounding soil. Choose a location well away from creeks, streams, and lakes—200 feet is generally recommended, though I find this figure is difficult to apply to anything other than lakes. (And keep in mind that reservoirs with highly fluctuating water levels are not, as most are named, lakes.) Canyons carved by flowing waterways have vastly different configurations. You can walk away from one for 3 miles and still remain in the flood plain, while with another you will need to climb two stories to find a secure spot.

The best plan is to stay above—well above—the high-water line of spring runoff. This line is not always easy to locate. In some terrain, the high-water line can be as elusive as the other sock—the one you swear went *into* the dryer. Though with a bit of training, you'll be able to find it.

The great springtime gush of water created by snowmelt usually brings down a load of debris: gravel, rocks, boulders, brush, limbs, even whole trees. Invariably, as flood waters peak, slow, and drop, portions of this debris become beached on open shores or caught in riparian vegetation, settling in a relatively horizontal line. In steep river canyons, as you float along on a late season water level, this line can be stories above your head. You might look skyward in mid-river and notice a tree trunk deposited curiously atop a house-size boulder, so high and dry by midsummer you'd guess only giants could have placed it there.

Another clue to the high-water line is a watermark—a bathtub ring—left as a horizontal stain on a canyon's rock walls. Some watercourses rage only in the spring or during flash floods from thunderstorms and are bone dry the remainder of the year. Learn to develop an eye for terrain and drainages—the low spots, the canyon bottoms, the erosion gullies, the dry washes. Ask knowledgeable locals to acquaint you with how high a river will rise during the spring runoff. Gradually, you'll learn to estimate the level fairly accurately from the shape and steepness of a canyon. When in doubt, climb higher; next year might be the cyclical big one—the twenty-five-year flood, the hundred-year flood.

Winter landscapes require more skill on our part. Spring's high-water line is obliterated under drifts of snow. Terrain is difficult to determine, and the chances of squatting on top of a buried streambed increase when you are not familiar with an area from previous summer visits. Steer clear of flat, open places, because they might be frozen ponds or wide meadows, the latter being a mountain's flood plains that gather and funnel water into creeks. The best advice is to head for the high ground. In deep snowpack or subzero temperatures, when you can't dig into the frozen earth or sometimes even dig far enough to find earth, the recommendation again is to pack-it-out.

The next and most thankful thing to learn about digging is that you're not required to dig to China. Quite the contrary: the most effective enzymes for breaking down excrement live within the top 8 inches of soil. It's generally recommended that you dig down 6 to 8 inches. This allows sufficient coverage of dirt to discourage animal contact and to keep flying insects from vectoring pathogens back to food areas.

Stirring is a brilliant technique that we all need to learn and employ. It is that "mixing" of the item we've deposited in our *one-sit hole* with loose dirt scraped from the sides of the hole before covering it over, all to the purpose of enhancing the decomposition rate by way of bringing soil bacteria into contact with a greater portion of the turd. Use a small stick for this purpose, something you can drop into the hole, not a tool you will be returning to your belt sheath or backpack. Think ahead. Pick up a downed stick along the way to your mission site, and when first digging the hole, loosen some dirt from the sides. Where there are no sticks, be creative. Use a stone. Carry a few Popsicle sticks you don't mind parting with. Be aware that "no sticks" might mean a high-use area that's been combed clean, an area with no bacteria in the soil, or an area with no soil—situations, once again, where packing-it-out is environmentally preferable to burying it.

The merits of stirring come to us as far back as 1982 in a study conducted in Montana's Bridger Range ("Potential Health Hazard from Human Wastes in Wilderness" by Kenneth L. Temple, Anne K. Camper, and Robert C. Lucas, *Journal of Soil and Water Conservation*, November-December 1982, Volume 37, Number 6). Fecal matter inoculated with bacterial pathogens *E. coli* and *Salmonella* was buried in cat holes. *Salmonella* proved a hardy survivor at all sites over the winter; *E. coli* persisted at some. The researchers theorized that fecal matter might actually insulate bacteria from the breakdown action of soil and proposed that mixing soil and feces might speed up die-off. But no one could imagine backcountry recreationists employing such a practice. Now here we are . . . closing in on a couple decades of stirring!

A trekker's urine is an altogether different item. Pee evaporates rapidly and is relatively sterile, unless a bladder infection is present (and a sufferer is well aware of such a condition). The major cautions with peeing are to keep away from high-use areas where the stench becomes unpleasant and to avoid peeing on gravel where urine will leave a lasting odor. In certain areas, notably Grand Canyon beaches, the National Park Service instructs people to pee directly into the river or on the wet sand at the water's edge. The pee is washed away by the daily fluctuations in water level created by Glen Canyon Dam upstream. These procedures were not adopted solely to eliminate rank urine smells; the concentration of pee (containing nitrogen) that boaters would otherwise deposit upon the soils of the Grand Canyon—an arid and slow-changing environment—would rapidly alter the soil chemistry and, in turn, the vegetation. The volume of river water in the Colorado, upwards of 15,000 cubic feet per second, also warrants this practice. Over the course of a year, that amounts to about one part pee to about fifty-five million parts water. Or, as once calculated by Mark Law, a National Park Service district manager, the equivalent of twenty-eight thousand cases of beer. Follow this procedure, however, only when the park or forest service specifically requests it.

For *any* type of eliminating, you should first wander a good distance from a camp area, not only for privacy but also to avoid squatting on potential sleeping spots or kitchen sites. If you are moving your camp every day, use this to advantage by making deposits in the areas of least visitation along your route. This is called elimination "on the move." Stay away from the edges of trails, which are in themselves high-use areas. Plan ahead, or you will find yourself skipping off the path to the first available nook—one that doubtless had the same appeal to many before you. Certain regions are predictably deep in shit, such as the shores just upstream of hellbender rapids. (Nothing can get bowels moving faster than thinking you're going to die.)

Let's focus for a moment on the subject of toilet paper; a rock climber once related the following story. While clinging to a ledge halfway up Yosemite's Half Dome, that urge we know so well suddenly came upon her. Rock climbing was then the least regulated of outback activities, and rock climbers were notorious for just letting it fly, bombs away! It wasn't uncommon to hear stories of climbers who'd been hit on the head. But in this instance, the climb was (as more and more are) organized to be respectful of the mountain and other climbers. Remaining safely in her leg loops, she skillfully peeled down her pants and positioned her carryout container. Next, she ripped off an arm's length of toilet tissue and then somehow lost her grasp of it and watched it quietly float away. The paper curled downward for only a moment before being snatched by an updraft. For the better part of an hour, soaring, diving, looping, happy as a mime artist, this tail of tissue entertained everyone strung across Half Dome. Need I say more about hanging on to your t.p.?

Actually yes, two more cautions. Don't bury it. Don't burn it. Burning was the accepted practice for some years, but the thinking has now changed. No matter how careful you think you might be, one accidental forest fire is one too many. Use as little paper, therefore, as you can manage, and then pack it all out. To better encourage this practice when camped with others, it's helpful to provide instructions and a discreet location for collection. A paper bag can be stationed at the outer edge of camp along with a shovel and a roll of t.p.

It goes without saying that you should also pack out all other inorganic accoutrements of toiletry: tampons, sanitary pads, and diapers. If you are washing diapers on a trip, dispose of the actual ca-ca in one-sit holes dug in the manner previously described. Haul the wash bucket above the high-water line and use only biodegradable soap. In rinsing out the wash bucket, use another pan or bucket to avoid rinsing directly in the stream. Pour the wash water into a hole (again, above the high-water line) and cover with dirt. Even with biodegradable soap, don't wash directly in a watercourse.

Digging a group latrine might be indicated on rare occasions. I cringe at the thought of sharing how to build latrines, and for that reason did not include it in the first edition of this book. Then more than several people inquired. With the idea that it is better for a person to have the best information and not use it than to ignorantly spade up random plots, I have laid it all out here— though not without considerable trepidation. Large, concentrated deposits of fecal matter break down extremely slowly. You mustn't head into the woods with the casual thought, *Oh, we'll just dig a big old pit*. Excavating a latrine will disturb a large area of plant life. In most places nowadays, a latrine will be environmentally inappropriate; you will need to come prepared to pack out all the human waste your group generates (again see chapter 3).

It is the highly unusual circumstance that requires a latrine. One situation comes to mind: I was recently reminded that there is an age, somewhere between infancy and adulthood, that's characterized by squeamishness and fits of giggling embarrassment. Usually groups of this maturity level remain close to base camp facilities. But if you find yourself in the boondocks as the leader of such a group, and you're not sufficiently assured that cat holes will be dug in a proper manner, then a latrine might be in order. When you're giving out instructions, keep in mind that embarrassment and squeamishness are cultural phenomena and will not disappear until adults become more direct in their own approach to the subject.

Think of a latrine as a multiperson cat hole, as opposed to a coffin-size trench. It needs to be easily accessible, closer to camp than a cat hole might be, and with some type of screening provided for privacy. The rest of the location considerations are similar to cat holes. Choose a spot a good distance from all water-courses and well above a river's high-water line. Stay far away from boggy areas, springs, meadows, and wetlands of any sort, and 200 feet from lakes. Keep out of dry washes that might carry storm runoff. In other words, again go for the high ground. Stop a minute, study the terrain, and visualize where water might flow. (Even in a desert water leaves signs: slick rocks are a giveaway, because water has probably polished them.)

Situate the latrine in soil with exceptionally good humus. The disadvantages of large deposits are a higher concentration of pathogens in one place and a slower rate of breakdown. Exca-vate a shallow (6- to 8-inch), narrow (8- to 10-inch) trench that people can straddle and squat over. To determine the length of your latrine, you must take into account the size of your group and the length of stay. Underestimate—you can always dig up a few more feet. Pile the dirt alongside the length of the trench. Instruct people to begin at one end; after each deposit, shovel in a dusting of soil, stir energetically, cover well, and tamp down. A communal stick for stirring can be conveniently left sticking into the used section of the trench, stirring end down. Ever hear of the expression "shit end of the stick"? This is the stick they were talking about. (In the old days, it had a rag attached to one end for cleaning chamber pots.) Finally, leave a paper bag handy to the squatter for refuse. Later it will be burned in the campfire or packed out.

In the end, we all have a decision to make about our sanitary methods. The procedure we choose will depend the size of our group, the maturity and agility of its members, the type of terrain, the season and climate, the remoteness of the location, the visitor volume, and on and on. The easier we make it for ourselves, the harder it will be on Mother Earth. For those of us who grew up on the "P.U.s!" of Western civilization's toiletries, it's going to require a fair portion of determination at some bends in the trail. But take heart: we're all learning together—about something we all do.

🪶

Ocean saltwater has long been considered a different story than fresh water. It's customary when sea kayaking to void in a can, toss the contents overboard, rinse out the can, and resume paddling. Or there's the option of jumping overboard, provided you are practiced in solo rescue and can haul yourself back in. On ecological grounds, some sea-touring groups have recommended water disposal, even for *number two*, over waiting for a beach disposal. There are boaters who'll argue that disposal of shit in water around island communities is safe when it's tossed into a moving, deep-water column of 12 feet or more. Yet the casual vacation kayaker (me) paddling in a maze of channels will find it difficult to ascertain depth beneath a bobbing boat. What's more, a knowledge of tides is involved or, instead of flushing out to sea, your "turd overboard" could wash right back onto favored clam beds.

The idea of *aqua dumps* or *shit-puts*, as they're called, runs contrary to all fibers of my being. Recollection of a water experience in Mexico reinforces my resistance. Someone once handed me a cheap ticket to Acapulco and I arrived on the lovely tropical beaches only to be warned not to swim in the bay's polluted waters. Too much raw sewage, it seemed. When the heat became oppressive, I swam in the hotel's pool—might as well have been side-stroking through chlorination at home.

By federal law, oceangoing vessels are prohibited from dumping sewage inside the 3-mile zone, from shore. A kayak is but a one-person/one-coffee-can yacht. With sea kayakers paddling our coasts in increasing numbers, typically touring close to islands and through small bays, or weaving through estuaries where wildlife viewing is best, it is this author's recommendation, on a planet already overburdened with excrement—and where we worry enough about such things as oil spills, balloons turning up in dead marine animals' intestines, the price of scallops—that fecal matter never be tossed overboard. But at least not inside the 3-mile zone of the mainland or the most seaward island in a group of islands. Packing-it-out, transporting it home for sewage treatment, is the preferred course of action. Second best—a cat hole dug in vegetation above the beach—is reasonable on occasion. There is no law that says sea kayakers can't set the example for the rest of the world. The ocean herself is saying, "Enough!"

So pack your trowel and container (see chapter 4) before setting out to sea like the Owl and the Pussycat in your beautiful pea-green boat.

3 When You Can't Dig a Hole

In days of old
When knights were bold
And toilets weren't invented
They left their load
Along the road
And walked off so contented.

—A childhood ditty; author unknown

In the pursuit of unknowns, a ranging world explorer can throw open entire new universes, not to mention some curious dimensions of toiletry and disposal. Sometimes there's just no place to dig a hole. Most of us never have occasion to pray that we won't have to go big potty outside when it's forty below or while dangling in midair between pitons on a thousand-foot rock face. In all probability, we are home knitting, walking the dog, or watching the Super Bowl. Of course, anyone trudging on foot to the South Pole or climbing Mount Everest is already committed to a multitude of unpleasantries. These breeds of outdoor enthusiasts are extraordinary souls; pride in their accomplishments does not spring from enduring the familiar. The morning constitutional behind the morning paper is an ordinary, even enjoyable, task when performed at home. But under adverse conditions, this simple activity can turn into a colossal calamity or feat of contortion.

Consider the mishap Chris Bonington endured at 26,000 feet during an ascent on Everest, as described in his book *The Ultimate Challenge* (New York: Stein & Day, 1963):

> Now we've got these one-piece down suits; it's not too bad, in fact it's comparatively easy to relieve oneself when wearing the down suit by itself. If, however, you are wearing the down suit and the outer suit, it is absolutely desperate, trying to get the two slits to line up. . . . Afterwards, without thinking, without looking back, I stood up and shoved my windproof suit back on. . . . I did not realize anything was wrong—until I poked my hand through the cuff! I tried to scrape it off—rub it off—but by this time the sun had gone, it was bitterly cold and it had frozen to the consistency of concrete.

Bonington is to be cheered for sharing his predicament; it provides solace, after the fact, for those in the misery-loves-company category, and it serves to forewarn the rest of us of one disastrous route to humiliation.

Next take note of this poor woman, who also bought a suit of misery. A robust friend of mine was camped on Oregon's Three Sister's during a blizzard, when an imperious peristaltic contraction indicated it was time to crawl out of the tent and squat. So, out she crawled into a complete whiteout, snow blowing horizontally on a wicked wind. Five layers of clothes had to be stripped from her rosy behind and shoved below her knees. Never mind the freezing; in retrieving her pants she found that each layer, not unlike a birdbath, had captured a supply of snow. Once the clothes were again clasped to her body, the snow began to melt. Winter campers call it the "soggies." When questioned as to whether she might not have some helpful hint for others caught in such circumstances, her only reply came, "Hold it!"

Two timeworn solutions to the undeniable problems associated with winter camping do offer themselves. Trapdoors decidedly provide some buttress against inclement weather. Fashioned after the old union suits with their fanny drop-flaps, various styles are available in heavy expedition wear. And the other merciful aid in subzero temperatures? Just what *did* great-grandma do when the weather was too bitter to pad along in her bare feet and flannel nightie to the outhouse? Of course, the old porcelain chamber pot—the "thunder mug," as it was called. Less elegantly, coffee cans have been used. And a variety of imaginative newer solutions will appear as we move through the next chapters.

Of course, not all extreme adventures issue forth from remote high and cold country. Another friend, an expedition leader, was once caught in rush-hour gridlock on the fourth level of a freeway interchange. It was, thankfully, only a *number one* emergency; he filled his thermos four times and casually dumped the contents out the window. From a reliable female source, I've heard that snap-shut plastic bread savers have been put to the same good use on long cross-country hauls across barren landscapes. Me? I'd rather pull to the shoulder, park my old pickup with it's tailgate angled slightly away from the highway (to provide cover from behind), then swing open the passenger door (blocking the view from oncoming traffic) and sit on what today suffices for a running board. Human ingenuity is a savior when you can't hold it for another minute.

But, along with ingeniousness, we also have our weaknesses, our blind spots, and our fastidious aversions to anything leaning toward fecal ickiness, which translates into a colossal calamity for Mother Earth. The numbers of both hardy explorers and casual backcountry travelers continue to swell around the globe, forcing us to grapple with the identical sanitation problems of T. J. Crapper's nineteenth century. Too much stuff, no good place for it to go. No matter how conscientious people become about carting back their trash and food garbage to major trailheads, each wave of visitors still leaves, in addition to footprints, shit. You can only cram so many apples into a barrel and then the barrel is full. And our dear Mother is screaming.

The ever-growing feeling in the outdoor community is that we can no longer afford—like knights of old—to leave our load along the road. In one example, grievously noticeable to early spring backpackers, is the turdly remains of the previous season's visitors. With the snow's melting, frozen lumpettes left by cross-country skiers sit plunk on top of the ground. The weather warms and they thaw and ripen along with the rest of the landscape. For the early hiker seeking a few days solace in untrammeled places, this is a horrific sight. One might better have stayed home and scheduled a tour of the local sewage treatment plant.

Sometimes, leaving behind even the most properly buried deposits can cause irreparable ecological damage. Small islands, for instance, have tenuous ecosystems at best. The fragility of islands is inherent: they have no adjacent support system. Off the coast of Maine lie three thousand islands, many no bigger than an isolated acre. The interdependence of life on an acre island—what looks to us to be grasses and a couple of trees—has been in the making for millions of years. Now visitors come, and not just in the form of the odd fisherman or lovers picnicking, but sea kayakers by the dozen camping overnight, or tour groups off chartered schooners, sometimes thirty at a time, stopping for a landside lunch. Too many cat holes, too much disturbed earth, and the grasses vanish, leaving topsoil to the mercy of wind and weather. It's far better for us to tread gently than to be confronted later on with another in the long line of mitigations—not always successful mitigations—that we now face.

The ecosystems of caves are another example of isolated and delicately balanced flora and fauna. Caves often shelter vulnerable and delightfully bizarre little creatures found nowhere else on earth. For the spelunker, in addition to the serious concern about survival of species interdependence, there is the compelling subject of rank odors. The true cave-lover looks on the removal of bodily waste as merely one step in heedful exploration.

A sensitive ecosystem that's not always so evident, even to those best informed, is the wetland. Washington State's King County touts a 100-page Sensitive Areas Ordinance that creates buffer zones of 25 to 100 feet around three different classifications of wetlands, ruling out, among other things, septic systems. The ordinance contains no specifications for an individual camper's deposits; nonetheless, local environmentally minded sea kayakers using cat-hole methods find occasion for the joke, "Know your wetland plants!" Not so easy, I was once told, by Ken Carrasco, a King County environmental educator. "Of all the environmentally sensitive areas, the most difficult to delineate and classify are wetlands." There, vegetation is not only the obviously swampy specimens like eelgrass and cattails, but also the trees of western red cedar, black cottonwood, and Sitka spruce that often inhabit "forested wetlands." Only seven days of inundation during the growing season (in the Seattle area, March to November) are necessary to set the stage for survival of a wetland species. And wetlands vary greatly in size, some taking up no more space than an office file cabinet. To quote a chapter heading from the Army Corps of Engineers' publication, *Wetland Plants of the Pacific Northwest*: "Wetland Identification Complexities: Life Is Not Simple."

"Packing-it-out"—the practice of capturing and transporting fecal matter and sometimes pee out of the backcountry—is nowadays the practical alternative to burial in high-use areas and fragile ecosystems. As early as 1988, Cal Adventures, the outdoor program at the University of California at Berkeley, under the direction of Rick Spittler, began experimenting with individual containerization systems for participants in their cross-country skiing program. CA's novel techniques were successful, if rudimentary: milk cartons with duct tape. Today on many busy trails, day hikers are given plastic "bags" for packaging up their turds and carrying them out. Conscientious sea kayakers, in many parts of the world, are paddling their solid eliminations home. The U.S. Forest Service straps portable toilets onto mules that accompany trail crews into the mountains. The big outdoor schools, Colorado Outward Bound and the National Outdoor Leadership School, teach packing-it-out. Even rock climbers (fed up with oversized hail?) are changing their ways. Mountaineers—where favorite routes are heavily traveled—have jumped on the clean wilderness effort. And Antarctic expeditions now pack-it-out. Every year, participation in this cleanup campaign is made easier by a changing overall consciousness—everybody in the same poo boat—and the development of specialized equipment. Not to mention tightening regulations. But now we'll temporarily leave the *individual* poop packer and turn our focus for the rest of this chapter to *groups*, and their portable shitarees.

Some forty years ago, whitewater boaters emerged as the first *parties* of wilderness travelers to experiment with hauling human feces out of pristine areas. River terrain poses a unique problem because overnight camping is confined by the naturally limited beaches of steep and narrow canyons or by adjacent privately owned land. When shooting rapids began to grow in popularity, the increased human visitation was subsequently followed by tremendous concentrations of fecal matter. The need to pack-it-out became evident when people began turning over others' "stuff" in an effort to bury their own.

Since 1979, all solid human excreta from Grand Canyon river trips has been containerized and removed. The River Permit Office for the Grand Canyon issues two full pages of instructions to trip leaders about packing-it-out. On Canyon beaches, there's the potential for 200,000 deposits per year, or roughly 50 tons of shit. Imagine, purely for the sake of comprehension, finding 200,000 helpings of spaghetti and meatballs buried in the sand. With that picture, the National Park Service's regulations become perfectly understandable. No trip is allowed on the river without ample approved holding tanks, proper education, and a commitment to leaving behind no human poop.

It wasn't long before these regulations spread to other heavily run rivers. When removal was adopted in 1983 on Idaho's Main Salmon (Lewis and Clark's famed River of No Return), Bob Abbott, who was then district ranger of Nez Perce National Forest, was nothing short of skeptical about public cooperation. As a second-generation ranger, born even in a ranger district, Abbott had spent years observing *Homo sapiens*' behavior in the wild. The Tin Can Tourist, as litterbugs were called in the days before plastic, couldn't be counted on to pack out even the smallest bits of trash. Abbott's reaction to the idea of expecting visitors to haul out their excrement was "You gotta be kidding! We'll have shit from hell to breakfast!" But soon he became a convert and then instrumental in promotion, getting a SCAT Machine (page 40) installed in Riggins, Idaho, near the Main Salmon's take-out. The other day, he emanated downright pride in saying, "You can visit a beach that's had seven thousand visitors in the space of two months [which is four thousand more than when this book's second edition appeared] and see no sign that humans have been there." Upon retirement, Abbott traveled to Washington, D.C., where he was presented with the award for Excellence in Wild River Management by then–Vice President Al Gore.

Packing-it-out suddenly got kicked upstairs when, in October 1993, in what turned out to be a momentous decision, the Environmental Protection Agency (EPA) outlawed dumping human fecal matter in landfills. Although not a law enacted with wilderness-goers in mind, it greatly and immediately affected us. As an EPA representative back then explained, "Sewage must go where it can be treated—into sewage treatment plants, sewers, or septic tanks."

Up to that point, the classic toilet system for river runners had been an inexpensive ($15) WWII ammunition can, commonly called an *ammo can* or *rocket box*, and easily acquired at most any surplus store. Their lids clamp down vicelike onto a rubber gasket that creates a secure seal against spillage. When in use, a can was lined with a plastic garbage bag, and a toilet seat positioned on top. Presto, outdoor potty! The toilet seat was often omitted on gear-light private trips, and that led to the nickname *groover*, from the parallel indentations left in a sitter's bum.

With recycled rocket boxes, boaters hauled literally thousands of pounds of human waste out of canyons. But always, awaiting them at take-outs was a big glitch—no facility equipped to receive bagged shit. Plastic bags, which don't biodegrade rapidly, are incompatible with septic tanks and sewage treatment plants. They particularly gum up the works in the honey wagons that pump out trailhead outhouses.

After caring for their cargoes of turds—painstakingly removing them from camps, ferrying them down rivers, bearing them across beaches, and packing them into vehicles—stymied rafters hurled a goodly percentage of those bulging bags into open pits on someone's south forty. At best, the bags were trucked for miles to a sewage treatment plant, where the contents were poured out and the soiled bags bagged again and dropped into the trash. At worst, and not uncommon, came the woeful tales of river guides who feared they were doomed to driving a vehicle permanently laden with the infamous bags. Many a moonless landscape, a handy Dumpster, or a lonesome spot on the road caught their share of "fling it and runs." Something was terribly awry when the most environmentally conscious bunch around—whitewater boaters—were stuck with no better solution.

The EPA, as many saw it, had come to the rescue. Its ruling, however inadvertently, confronted the big void (pun intended) in sewage facilities at take-outs and trailheads. It served to force progress beyond plastic garbage bags, because even if you were to pour the fecal matter down the pipe at an RV station, you still had to contend with the soiled bag. Not everyone had the iron stomach required to launder one. So, what followed was a brainstorming all around that continues to this day.

$\clubsuit$

The giant **SCAT Machine**, designed by wizard river guide John Witzel, is the overall marvel. It's essentially an industrial-size dishwasher hooked into a sewer system, and it empties and cleans most any portable, reusable backcountry toilet. The washer will neatly dump 5-gallon buckets, box-type potties, even your septic tank if you can dig it out of the ground, but indeed anything with at least an 8-inch top opening and a recommended minimum height of 13 inches (containers $11^3/_4$ to 12 inches tall work marginally, but anything shorter doesn't empty properly). Just bring your full container and your own strapping to secure it. Remove the container's lid, and place it on the accessory wash rack. Closing the machine will cause it to swing through a one-eighty turn and ship your holding tank's contents down the sewer. Drop in a few quarters or tokens and the apparatus washes and sanitizes your tank and all but reaches out and hands it back to you.

Installation sites for a standard SCAT Machine require an existing sewer, septic, or leach line system, a 220-power source, and a water supply capable of 10 gallons per minute. Depending on bells and whistles, prices range from $21,000 to $50,000, including delivery and installation within 350 miles of the manufacturer, with additional mileage extra. Witzel has decked out washers with alarms—one automatically phones its owner when the machine needs attention—and fashioned models that are solar powered and trailer mounted. The latter require a "nursing" unit that comes out periodically to pump out the sewage and resupply the fresh water. The higher-end prices cover items such as attached grinders and solar panels. "I haven't equipped any with a drink holder yet!" he laughs. SCAT Machines generally sell to federal agencies (Bureau of Land Management, U.S. Forest Service, National Park Service) or to a group of commercial outfitters. They serve mostly river runners in their locations at Meadview, Arizona; Asotin, Washington; Riggins and North Fork, Idaho; and at Maupin, Heritage Landing, and Foster Bar, Oregon. The SCAT at the marina in Priest Lake, Idaho, is for campers returning from the islands. Witzel will custom build a machine to wash any particular container. (**SCAT Machine** • **www.scatmachine.com** • Frenchglen Blacksmiths • 39269 Highway 205 • Frenchglen, OR 97736 • Phone: 541-495-2315 • Email: info@scatmachine.com)

🌷

At the BLM office in Baker City, Oregon, Kevin McCoy is the outdoor recreation manager and also heads up river rangers on the designated Wild & Scenic stretches of the Grande Ronde, the Wallowa, and the Powder. He and his lead river ranger, Kevin Hoskins, have been involved now for twenty years in backcountry human waste management, watching regulations stiffen, while they've nudged along experimental pack-it-out systems, once buying nearly everything on the market in order to acquaint their rangers with the different products. Meanwhile, the use of public lands was tripling and federal agencies weren't able to keep up with the expense of maintaining enough toilet facilities. When in 2000, the Grande Ronde corridor shifted to "mandatory" packing-it-out, McCoy saw it as an opportunity to place stewardship, more appropriately, in the lap of users—rivers runners, ATVers, and horse packers.

At first, he faced unwilling participants. A party of river runners coming off a five-day trip showed up at the take-out with an empty potty and bald-faced claims that "No one had to go." But nowadays, he has a huge success story. Over the years, McCoy's rangers have evolved from the lousy chore of trail and campsite cleanup—that is, picking up clumps of shit and toilet paper with salad tongs—to happily noticing they are engaged in commonplace conversations with the public about the care of excreta. And getting compliance. "The no-way-you're-going-to-make-*me*-crap-in-a-bucket folks" McCoy cheers, "are carrying around facilities in their vehicles." And all it took was a bucket—of the ordinary 5-gallon hardware-store variety—with a couple minor accessories and a small bag of potting soil. Plus, of course, a group of dedicated, well-versed rangers comfortable with toilet talk. And a system that's monumentally user-friendly and inexpensive. (See Do-It-Yourself Soil Can, the Baker City BLM's do-it-yourself system, on page 52)

But the Kevins' system is only an example of what has transpired. As might be guessed—with new frontiers and creativity the adventurer's eternal callings—rising to the occasion of the EPA ruling came a spate of inventors, all scurrying to produce a washable, reusable container that was also user-friendly—as in, requiring the least holding of the nose. For a while, a new design appeared almost every week. Now there's been a settling out, with some models disappearing and others taking hold.

There *is* one alternative—in case you're wondering—to all this lugging around of poop. Though not something I personally recommend, I present it here and leave it for you to decide. The suggestion arrived in one of the many letters I receive—a correspondent I've since duly dubbed the Enema Man. In a short typed note, he graciously shared his practice of holing up in a motel to flush his colon the night before striking out on a weekend of fishing. This enables him to roam about untroubled by the particulars of how to squat in the woods, leaving him to concentrate solely on his sport, while—he writes in all sincerity—simultaneously "avoid[ing] polluting the streams and their environs." If this appeals to you, read no further. Hand this book to a neighbor! The rest of us, though now equipped with the knowledge that here might very well lie the solution to a world of problems, will, nonetheless, move on to examining holding tanks.

I list (beginning on page 46) the manufacturers of washable, reusable, backcountry toilets because most are small operations, and it seems certain that encouraging their use is uppermost in the cosmic plan. Although I've added a few comments about each model, this is not meant to be an exhaustive evaluation; design revisions occur frequently and, to be fair, I have not climbed onto all of them. The very act of plopping down on one reveals a critical characteristic—how readily the toilet tips over. And this, believe me, is important. Once a contraption containing the crap of fourteen people throws you to the ground and tries to drown you, there's a good chance you'll turn into a couch potato for life.

When purchasing a portable toilet, there are numerous things to watch for and weigh. Pick and choose the design features that most suit you. You can't have everything with the cheaper models, but sometimes you don't need everything. Off the top, there are four important things to consider: your health, container stability, "disgust factor," and price. Starting with the last and simplest, current prices range from $15 to $587. Following the general discussion, they are presented from high end to low, along with the do-it-yourself Soil Can and the few companies that offer rentals.

Handling toilets is not a business to be taken lightly, and any potential for direct exposure to fecal matter during the setting up, packing up, emptying, or cleaning processes should be carefully considered. Wearing latex gloves is suggested when drawing the short straw for potty duty—a wise precaution, but also one lamentably ironic. Proud as we are about diminishing our consumption of plastic bags, we seem to be tying our next Gordian knot around a mountain of latex gloves. The alternative is a good soap-and-water scrub. Health is definitely the priority for the clean-out staff.

Some holding tanks, upon opening, will "burp in your face." Methane gas is a natural by-product of anaerobic decomposing feces. Be forewarned: a sealed holding tank—full or partially full—left in the sun can blow up. Fireworks of that caliber have the potential to psychologically brand a person for life. Short of actual explosion, tanks can also bubble and cough and emit world-class farts. Having an automatic pressure-release mechanism is a decided advantage on long or hot-weather trips. If yours is a courageous spirit, however, tanks without pressure-release valves are generally cheaper and you can crack the lid occasionally, remembering to pack your gear so the lid is accessible. Be advised that peeing in the potty contributes to methane buildup, but not peeing in it can make the dumping difficult at trip's end.

There are two schools of thought on content consistency: the wet and the dry. The wet group believes in brewing a sort of slurry that will easily pour. Thus sometimes women on the trip are instructed to pee in the pot, and other times, all guests are told to pee elsewhere, while the guides discreetly monitor and maintain a proper consistency. The dry group is acutely aware that liquids add to weight and prefers to collect only solid waste, adding water at the completion of a trip.

Next to ponder is shape: round, square, or oblong. A round object, if not entirely sturdy, can eventually assume a square shape when squished by dunnage. Consider your load—that is, how your gear is packed. Also, a bucket, with its top larger in diameter than its bottom, offers less sitting stability than a container of squatter and squarer design.

Other high priorities are sturdiness of construction material and top-of-the-line seals at all the openings. If a boat flips in a "mother" rapid, there should be no chance of a holding tank leaking during "maytagging" at the bottom of a sous hole. Seals must pass what I'm now calling the Donnie Dove Test, giving DDT a whole new meaning. Dove is Canyon REO's (River Equipment Outfitters) expert on leakage. A man with a purpose, he packs a gallon of water seemingly wherever he goes, pouring it into the latest inventions and turning them upside down. Dove espouses a simple but profound axiom: If it can't hold water, it shouldn't hold shit! At last count, not all passed his test. One more thing to be said about material is that plastics more readily absorb odors than do stainless steel and aluminum, but any container when used regularly will take on a whiff. To help, toss a half-cup of baking soda into cleaned tanks that are sitting around between trips.

Eventually, you must think about the end of your trip and the task of dumping the holding tank. Compatibility with the SCAT Machine is a plus when you are planning to be near one of the few on the planet, but compatibility with RV dumping stations is a *must*. The latter is achieved by attaching a garden hose at one opening, a sewer hose at another, and blasting fresh water through the tank. Some tanks are not equipped with orifices that fit a freshwater hose. The flushing is instead accomplished through the larger toilet-seat hole, which can produce unsanitary splash back. You can remedy that, somewhat, by fashioning a large rubber washer through which you insert the hose. Or clean it at home without the power wash.

Sewage cleaning services come highly recommended as a way of entirely avoiding the clean-out chore. With this news, I called around the rural areas where I live and found no such service. I was, in fact, alarmed to discover that the portable plastic outhouses, the ones seen lined up at all manner of public events, were cleaned merely with squirts of cold water. Towns near takeouts for popular river runs are probably better bets. In any case, it's worth the call—if nothing else, it might inspire someone to propose an updating of public health standards. Another choice for disposal is a sewage treatment plant. There the contents of a holding tank are poured through an open grate, but mucking out the container is left to you.

If your group is large or your trip long, you will need more than one holding tank. When calculating volume, be sure to allow for not only actual space but also what is termed "disgust factor." Using the same container for more than two or three days, or until topped off, will gag almost anyone; in classic approach/avoidance conflict mode, most of us will instinctively peer down the hole before sitting. In addition, there are the critical matters of tidal waves, splash back, and for gentlemen, the safety of those forever dangling darlings. Prized is the toilet-seat mounting that provides for perching well above the can's contents. Deodorizers, or sweeteners as they're called, can also help minimize disgust factor.

The prices I've quoted are retail and don't include shipping. Any dimensions given are for holding tanks alone—sometimes inside measurements, sometimes outside—without a seat assembly on top. Ammo cans and rocket boxes are designated in millimeters, which refers to the type of ammunition originally stored in them, not the size of the can: for instance, a 30mm is smaller than a 25mm.

Another term to know is *user-day*; this means one person, one day. In other words, 50 user-days could mean five people shitting for ten days or ten people shitting for five days, or even fifty people shitting for one day. Capacities noted are not calculated by any standardized method, but given in accordance with the manufacturer's advertising. Some are for poops per can, some for people per day no matter what they are eating, and some for full-to-the-brim tanks.

Try as I might, I found it difficult to establish the size of an "average" poop. In medical encyclopedias there is a hesitancy to commit to a one-figure average, the worldwide range of normalcy being broad. Anyone who takes a dump three to twenty-one times per week can be considered normal. The individual product is dependent on a person's age, size of physical frame, diet, gender, race, continent of residence, even personality. People who eat more fiber produce more bulk. Men, as a rule, produce more than women. A typical stool in India weighs three times that of one in England or the United States, whereas in Uganda (where surely they eat bricks!) turd poundage is five times greater.

Those of us who survived the 1960s pledged to the eternal process of "getting our shit together," might be surprised to learn that though our shit might stink less now, it probably weighs more; the fifth edition of *Gastrointestinal Disease: Pathophysiology, Diagnosis, Management* by Sleisenger and Fordtran (Philadelphia: W. B. Saunders, 1993), tells us that people with high self-esteem produce heavier stools. Thankfully, Carol Hupping Stoner takes a stab at averages for us in *Goodbye to the Flush Toilet: Water-Saving Alternatives to Cesspools, Septic Tanks, and Sewers* (Emmaus, PA: Rodale Press, 1977), calculating daily human excrement at $1/2$ pound, moist weight. That should help—the half-pounder being now a worldwide institution.

A little more advice? Carry a gallon of water and ask a lot of questions.

Washable-Reusable, Carry-Out Toilet Systems

Jon-ny Partner ■ www.partnersteel.com ■ Partner Steel Company ■ 3187 Pole Line Road ■ Pocatello, ID 83201 ■ Phone: 208-233-2371 ■ Email: camp@partnersteel.com

The **Jon-ny Partner** ($587) is what many call the Cadillac of portable toilets, a bombproof, stainless steel holding tank. The price includes the tank with an automatic pressure-release valve, a transport lid with rubber gasket and collar clamp, a toilet seat with a lid, and a flush kit (a clamp-on funnel, equipped with a $3/4$-inch opening for a garden hose, an inside sprayer, and a sewer hose) for RV dumping stations. The Jon-ny Partner is also compatible with the SCAT Machine. Dry weight is 20 pounds (90 when full) and capacity is 50 to 60 user-days—calculated at 27 cubic inches per person, per day, and based on a study of boaters who ate such things as pork chops and omelets for breakfast! Stout handles at seat level and a square design (12 x 12 x 17 inches), assure stable seating. The toilet seat has a flange that fits down inside the box and provides additional stability when in use, but many require cleaning before packing away. River outfitters, catering to classy clients, will sometimes bring enough Partners to open a new one every day. Sold mostly to commercial and private whitewater boaters and hunting parties for base camps. The Forest Service in Alaska and Idaho packs them in with trail crews. Customizing is welcomed; ask for Bill Roskelley.

Human Waste Tank ■ Waterman Welding ■ 2552 South Highway 89A ■ Kanab, UT 84741 ■ Phone: 435-644-5729 ■ Email: wweld@expressweb.com

The **Human Waste Tank** ($292.60), made of marine-grade, corrosion-resistant aluminum, will withstand heavy use and abuse from its acidic contents. The standard size (14 x 21 x 12 inches tall) fits in the same space as two 20mm ammo cans. Comes with an automatic pressure-release valve and a 3-inch clean-out drain, a transport cap with a lock ring, a seat mount, and top handles that don't interfere with adjacent gear. The 1-inch-diameter top hole and 3-inch-high collar make it SCAT Machine compatible. Flush apparatus ($108), for emptying at RV dumping stations, includes an inverted funnel (with a $3/4$-inch garden hose fitting) that secures to the tank with the transport cap's lock ring. You must buy your own sewer hose, clamp, and toilet seat. Spare tanks are available ($226.60). Dry weight is 12 pounds, with a capacity of 64 user-days. And a determined, noncommercial group of ten, I was told, could get by on one tank for as long as ten days (or 100 user-days). Custom building, any size to suit you, ask for Scott Dunn.

Attached to the Human Waste Tank is a remarkable bit of history. A river guide in the Grand Canyon before packing-it-out became regulation, Scott Dunn was one of the first to promote containerization. He remembers the Park Service landing at his camp more than thirty-six years ago on one of their routine inspections just when he was experimenting with an ammo can and a plastic bag. "They gave me not such good grades on canyon descriptions," he says, "but rated me right up at the top on human waste." The Human Waste Tank was originally designed in 1972, by Ron Smith of Grand Canyon Expeditions who was ahead of his time with a washable, reusable container.

ECO-Safe ■ **www.eco-safe.net** ■ GTS, Inc. ■ 4037 East English Street ■ Wichita, KS 67218 ■ Phone: 785-505-1482 ■ Email: pabecker@aol.com

The **Eco-Safe** Ammo Box System ($164.95), 17 x $7^1/_2$ x $13^1/_2$ inches tall, is a molded tank designed to fit inside a 20mm surplus ammo can, giving double protection against spillage and odor. It can also be used as a stand-alone system (see Harness below). Equipped with a 6-inch screw-top lid; a 3-inch drain hole and 4-foot flexible drain hose; a $^3/_4$-inch flush hole and $^3/_4$-inch garden-hose-to-box adapter; plugs for both holes; and a separate raised toilet-seat assembly with lid. Dry weight (tank only) is $5^1/_4$ pounds. Accommodates 50 user-days. Sells mostly to commercial and private rafters. Ammo Box Spare Tank ($109.95). The Ammo Box Harness ($36.00), nylon webbing and D-rings, is for carrying the stand-alone tank and lashing it into rafts.

The Boom Box System ($119.95), $13^1/_2$ x 9 x 8 inches, with its $2^1/_2$-gallon tank and self-storing seat, is the right size for canoes and sea kayaks. It comes with the same fittings, hoses, plugs, and wrench as the larger Ammo Box. Dry weight is $2^1/_2$ pounds; good for 20 user-days. Boom Box Spare Tank ($79.95). See page 64 for the solo Clean Mountain Can.

All ECO-Safe tanks are made of high-density polyethylene, with rounded corners for easy cleaning, and outfitted with a pressure-release vent in the lids. Compatible with RV dumping stations and the SCAT Machine.

D-Can ■ www.canyonreo.com ■ Canyon REO ■ P.O. Box 3493 ■
Flagstaff, AZ 86003 ■ Phone: 800-637-4604 ■ Email:
info@canyonreo.com

Canyon REO's **D-Can** ($188), also called BP-Can for bombproof,
is a retrofitted surplus ammo can. New—as in, never employed
before as a toilet—the 25mm cans ($17^1/_2$ x 10 x $14^1/_2$ inches tall)
are $2^1/_2$ inches wider and more stable than the 20mm and 1 inch
wider than the 30mm. D-Cans come coated inside with an easily
cleaned polyurethane "rhino lining" and fitted with a welded top/
seat opening. A double safety seal on the transport lid is "Donnie Dove" guaranteed not to leak. The can is not equipped with a
pressure-release valve and you must buy your own sewer hose and
toilet seat. An "optional design," same price, has a toilet seat with
a flat-closing lid that's mounted on a slide-on aluminum top for use
just in camp. Both cans are SCAT Machine compatible, and for an
additional $10, you can have a receptacle installed that accepts a
sewer hose for cleaning at RV dumping stations. The freshwater
flush is accomplished through the 10-inch-diameter seat opening,
or, with the optional design, through the $17^1/_2$ x 10-inch opening.
Dry weight is 26 pounds, with a capacity of 70 to 80 user-days
("hero use" up to 100). You can also rent D-Cans for $2 per day.
And the best: for a measly $20, at the end of your trip, you are
allowed to return a chockfull can to Canyon REO, turn your back,
and walk away.

Coyote Bagless Toilet Systems ■ www.riversports.com ■

Four Corners River Sports ■ 360 South Camino del Rio ■ Durango,
CO 81301 ■ Phone: 800-426-7637 ■ Email: info@riversports.com

The **Coyote Toilet** ($159.95) is a wide-based box (12 x 12 x 14
inches tall) of high-density polyethylene, with rounded corners
for easy cleaning. It comes with a 10-inch screw-top lid with gas-
ket, a 3-inch drain hole and 4-foot flexible drain hose, a $^3/_4$-inch
flush hole and $^3/_4$-inch garden-hose-to-box adapter, plugs for both
holes, and a separate raised fiberglass toilet seat (without lid). The
screw-top lid serves as the seat cover while in camp. A lip around
the top of the box provides a means for carrying. An Accessory

Tie-down System ($7.95), for nesting the box and lid and lashing it into rafts, also allows for carrying by the webbing. Spare box ($104.95). Replacement seat ($32.95). Dry weight is 9 pounds and capacity 55 user-days. Compatible with RV dumping stations and the SCAT Machine, but minus a pressure-release valve. The big pluses: Coyote Toilet has a lightweight, stable design and the price is right.

GO Anywhere Portable Toilet & Toilet Kits (aka **Pett Toilet & Wag Bags**) ▪ **www.gocleanwaste.com** ▪ Cleanwaste ▪ 290 Arden Drive ▪ Belgrade, MT 59714 ▪ Phone: 877-520-0999 ▪ Email: info@gocleanwaste.com

The **GO Anywhere Portable Toilet** ($116.95), used with GO Anywhere Toilet Kits ($39.95 for 12-pack), has a 14-inch-tall three-legged frame—making it stable on uneven ground—with a seat like a standard toilet. It will support 500 pounds and folds to the size of a briefcase, with handle. Weighs 7 pounds. The toilet comes with three of the Kits, which are double-bagging systems of biodegradable plastic, preloaded with Poo Powder, a non-toxic proprietary substance. Poo Powder also comes in bulk for extending the use of a bag, or using in your own bags. River and horse-packing groups may want to store full bags for carry-out in a rocket box. There's a 7-pound Privacy shelter ($162.95) and a Backpack ($76.95) that's set up to carry the entire system. For a lot more information on Poo Powder and GO Anywhere Kits for solo use, see page 60.

RESTOP ▪ **www.restop.com** ▪ American Innotek, Inc. ▪ 2320 Meyers Avenue ▪ Escondido, CA 92029 ▪ Phone toll free: 800-366-3941; or 760-741-6600 ▪ Email: info@whennaturecalls.com

The **RESTOP Commode** ($115) is a 5-gallon bucket made of thick-walled heavy-duty polyethylene that resists becoming brittle and cracking in temperatures of extreme cold or becoming soft in extreme heat. This is *not* the generic 5-gallon paint or pickle bucket—it's been tested by the U.S. Marine Corps with 300 pounds of pressure over 10 hours. Included in the price are a tight-sealing screw-on lid (Gamma Lid) with a gasket, a flexible foam toilet seat, and a 10-pack of RESTOP 2s, "bag-within-a-bag" systems containing a proprietary blend of super absorbent polymers and natural enzymes for disposing of human poop and pee. The outer bag is made of gas-impervious Mylar, for containing odor. Used bags (in line with EPA guidelines) can be tossed out with the regular trash. On the website is a slide-show demonstration of all the RESTOP products. Offered also is a 7$\frac{1}{2}$-pound Privacy Tent ($99) for convenient commode use in base camps.

The RESTOP portable dry toilet system was employed two years in a row on the Eco Everest Expedition (an annual trip organized by Asian Trekking—in conjuction with the Cash for Trash and the Cleaning Up Everest programs—that brings down garbage and human waste and tries out new eco-equipment). The RESTOP system is also approved by the National Park Service for Grand Canyon river trips. The bags have been recently adopted in Tatransky National Park in Poland, primarily for caving trips. See page 63 for solo use of RESTOP 2, without the commode, and for RESTOP 1 (a disposable urine bag) and RESTOP 2W (a kit that comes with a mesh transport bag).

Luggable Loo and **Double Doodie Toilet Waste Bags** ■ Reliance Products ■ 1093 Sherwin Road ■ Winnipeg, Manitoba ■ R3H 1A4 Canada ■ Phone (for wholesale orders): 800-665-0258

The **Luggable Loo Toilet Seat and Bucket** ($17.99) includes a 5-gallon plastic bucket with a snap-on toilet-seat-with-lid. Or purchase the toilet-seat-with-lid alone ($12.99) which will snap on and off any 5-gallon utility bucket. Use the Loo with Double Doodie Bags ($14.99 for 6-pack), which are double plastic bagging systems with proprietary Bio-Gel, "similar to what's in baby diapers."

Reliance Products also manufacture the Hassock Portable Toilet ($29.98). Both toilets are regaled as economical options mostly for car/tent camping, because they lack the tight-sealing transport lids needed for activities involving more jouncing around. The Double Doodie Bags, however, can be used without the commodes, by spreading them directly on the ground. For more discussion on the bags, see page 63.

Zölzer Aufblasbare Mobiltoilette ■ **www.zoelzer.de** ■ Heinz Zölzer, GmbH ■ Kupferdreher Str. 196 ■ D 45257 Essen-Kupferdreh, Germany ■ Phone: +49 (0) 201 48 78 15 ■ Email: marketing@zoelzer.de

The **Mobiltoilette** ($80) is a stack of three bright yellow inflatable rings (7.02-inch inside diameter; 17.16-inch outside diameter) that create a seat upon which to poop or pee. Add another ring if you want it taller. The top ring holds a single-use German "PE-bag." Use with a comfy stool, and it could be coupled with any of the above double-bagging products, weighs $10\frac{1}{2}$ ounces. Packed size: 21.06 x 3.9 x 2.34 inches. Call or email Susanne Reichelt (she speaks English) for prices and anything else I couldn't translate.

🌿

Now for a moment's recognition of the company that coined the words we so universally toss around: the Porta Potti. Manufactured by the Thetford Corporation, the Porta Potti is an integral seat/tank assembly with a handle and pour spout. Though dandy for RVs, trailers, and boats, it was not designed for river rafting or backcountry travel, as its water/chemical flush system adds to the weight while diminishing the capacity. Nor was the Porta Potti designed for the rigors of those sports, because without an additional securely sealing transport container, leakage could be a problem. Several sizes are available at discount stores. The smallest version ($5\frac{1}{4}$ x 14 x 15 inches tall) weighs $9\frac{1}{2}$ pounds and holds 2.6 gallons of fresh water with a holding tank capacity of 4.3 gallons that boasts 45 flushes.

🌿

Do-It-Yourself Soil Can

The **Soil Can** ($15 to $25), dreamed up and promoted by Oregon BLM's Kevin McCoy and Kevin Hoskins, will comply with regulations in many backcountry areas. Gather together a 5-gallon plastic bucket from a paint or hardware store and a Gamma Seal Lid (which is a screw-on that fits a 12-inch-diameter pail, is leak-proof, easy on the fingernails, and comes in a variety of bright colors, starting at $6.57 online), along with any old toilet seat, one carabiner, and a bag of potting soil. You can even beg a bucket from a local deli or restaurant; green pickle pails were the standard river rat bailing bucket before the emergence of self-bailing boats. Then follow these simple instructions: prime the bucket with 2 inches of potting soil and after each deposit throw in another fistful or two. Solids and paper go in the bucket, pee in the bushes, or in the river. With the carabiner, clip the wire handle onto your gear. The handle is the outfit's weak link, but a safety strap of nylon webbing is easily fashioned. Capacity? Well, a party of seven reportedly didn't half-fill a pail in three days. A shorter hardware-store version (2½ gallons) is better suited to mini-cats and inflatable kayaks. For a longer lasting bucket, consider the RESTOP 5-Gallon Commode Bucket (see page 50), with its accompanying Gamma Lid and foldable foam seat ring. All in all, there is nothing better than the Soil Can: it's low-cost, lightweight, about the same comfortable height as a home toilet, all organic, not yucky to peer into, not odoriferous (adding urine is what produces the knock-you-over smell—although some women, by nature, will be adding some pee to the bucket), self-floating if it gets away, doesn't muck up the inside wall even with jostling. The Soil Can is compatible with the SCAT Machine, or, at a trailhead, it's conveniently dumped into a vault toilet. Take your empty bucket home, swab it out with your toilet brush, and it's ready for the next trip. Soil Cans are currently employed by boaters, horse packers, and ATVers. Some folks have grown so fond of their Soil Can they've been seen temporarily trucking it off to a spot with a spectacular view.

Oregon's BLM is beginning to modify their vault toilets, adding a dump chute just for Soil Cans. The Soil Can is now the only system McCoy and Hoskins recommend, because "they've been flawless." Next time you're headed to a backcountry place where mandatory packing-it-out hasn't hit yet, take along a bucket anyway. Try it! Feel righteous! You'll like it! And so will the landscape.

The other great joy is that Soil Cans are only one step short of being the perfect system—which can be accomplished by adding the practice of composting their contents in your backyard or, perhaps someday, at a small facility near trip's end. Interested? Then switch from potting soil to peat moss (the former is inert, while the latter helps with breakdown). And thumb back to page xiv for a description of Joseph Jenkins's splendid volume *The Humanure Handbook: A Guide to Composting Human Manure.*

Rentals

D-Cans

See product description on page 49.

Professional River Outfitters (PRO) Ammo Cans ■ www.proriver .com ■ PRO, Inc. ■ 2800 West Route 66 ■ Flagstaff, AZ 86001 ■ Phone: 800-648-3236 ■ Email: info@proriver.com

PRO rents the traditional World War II 20mm ammo cans to permit holders of noncommercial Grand Canyon river trips. For $2 per day (picked up in Flagstaff), you receive the ammo can, a toilet seat mounted on a flange that covers the top of the can, and a seat riser. Capacity is 50 to 60 deposits. Additional ammo cans rent for 50 cents per day. For those who already own 20mm ammo cans, PRO will sell you the toilet seat assembly ($65) and the seat riser ($65). At almost any surplus store, you can purchase an ammo can for $10 to $15 and be the proud owner of a piece of American history—in fact, several histories. Inspect the gasket to make certain it's in good shape and will be watertight: don't guess, test it. Bruce Helin, owner of PRO and longtime rafter, recommends marking the cans and lids so "they can be kept together in the same orientation for best sealing." Ammo cans are SCAT Machine compatible; they can be dumped at sewage treatment plants, or you can buy a funnel that will allow you to pour the contents down the pipe at an RV dumping station. In the latter two cases you are stuck with manually cleaning the can. But when renting from PRO, the dumping and sterilizing chore is, literally, taken off your hands for as little as $20 per can.

The Baño • www.bikeraft.com • Holiday River Expeditions • 544 East 3900 South • Salt Lake City, UT 84107 • Phone: 800-624-6323 • Email: holiday@bikeraft.com

The **Baño** rents from Holiday River Expeditions only to non-commercial river trips on Green River's Desolation Canyon and Colorado's Cataract Canyon. Make arrangements through Holiday's Salt Lake City office and then pick one up in the town of Green River. With a name befitting its southwest origins, The Baño is a molded plastic holding tank (same material as giant-size garbage cans) with aluminum handles, stainless steel fasteners, a hard plastic seat assembly, and automatic pressure release. The lid and box mesh together in a tapered manner with a lock-down clamp. The tank is a stable design (14 x 17 x 12^{1}/$_{2}$ inches tall), slightly smaller than two 30mm rocket boxes. It weighs 15.1 pounds when totally assembled, and has a capacity of 50 user-days. Rents for $30 (one to three days), $50 (four to seven days), $2 per day thereafter, and $5 for the seat assembly. Price includes dumping and cleaning.

Since I first began writing about wilderness and shit, the practice of packing-it-out has moved from rivers, up mountainsides, across deserts, and out onto oceans. The number of people inspired to invent and willing to adopt removal techniques is astounding. Chapter 4 offers another set of technological advances. I sense we're not far from a marketable sonic Crap-Zapper with the capacity to instantly alter the molecular structure of a human turd. Imagine! A Trekkie phaser gun for the mountain trekker! Poop and poof?

4 Plight of the Solo Poop Packer

Everyone, at some time, is a continent of one.
—Pico Iyer, *Falling Off the Map*

You cannot escape. Every day a part of you turns to shit.
—Dan Sabbath and Mandel Hall, *End Product: The First Taboo*

Now for a walk on the wild side. Admittedly, the concept of carting around warm poo in a backpack is not just revolutionary; it is, on initial take, repulsive. To spirit us past the involuntary "gak!" reaction, a kind of higher inspiration is called for. We could envision the whole procedure as one of the marvels of physics—the shrinkage of the food supply as the shit container fills—matter into matter, a perfect example of Einstein's $E = mc^2$. Or we could take heart from Japan's renowned mountaineer, Junko Tabei, a woman animated far beyond her small frame. I watched her bound to the podium at an international toilet symposium, "Toilets and the Environment," in Toyama in 1996. With words fairly effervescing from every limb of her body, she related her mountaineering experiences, and, in particular, the burnished beauty of Antarctica that spurred her not to leave the blot of her own elimination on the scenery. Instead, she scooped it into a plastic bag, and tied it to the outside of her pack. The package froze, and in its thwacking to and fro to the rhythm of her gait (until she could prop it on a sled) served to invigorate her inner sense of being. When a person deals this intimately with her own shit, her soul melds seamlessly with Nature's.

Jim Wilson, another longtime mountaineer and a writer and the original proprietor of Pipestone Mountaineering in Missoula, Montana, recently told me over lunch a story of his own intimacy. I relay it here largely as inspiration for anyone needing courage to deal with poop collection. Even the newest products on the market wouldn't have provided much help for Jim, nor his climbing partner, Jim. In 1997, the two Jims were forging a new route up the east face of Denali. They had reached Harper Glacier, at 16,000 feet (minus 40°F), and were aiming for the summit when a storm blew up. Hurrying to pitch their itty-bitty tent next to an offset crevasse for shelter, they crawled in—not knowing they'd be tarrying in such extreme confines for ten days. Without space for much more than sleeping bags, and with the bulk of their gear outside, they managed to eat, hydrate, sleep, and keep up their spirits. The wind ripped 100 to 200 mph; the tent rattled and shuddered. Airborne pebbles off nearby exposed rock sandblasted the walls. Cold—so cold that if they stepped outside, even in all their clothes, they almost flash froze.

Then, as it has to eventually, push came to shove and Wilson thought to line a helmet with a plastic bag. That *his* helmet was the only one in the tent was his first surprise. Worse, because a helmet's shape is inherently round and the Jims didn't dare make any sort of mess, everything got up close and personal fast—each one holding the helmet for the other. The easy part turned out to be abiding by the approved designation for glacial disposal: crack open the tent flap and lob the bag into the crevasse. Two determined Jims made it to the summit and in descending on the standard route were able to bum food, but Wilson lost fifty pounds in forty-five days and required a six-month recovery.

. Wilson's spontaneous generosity in sharing this story, with its obvious humiliation, and then agreeing to my printing it, makes me chagrin to complain a smidgeon, ever, about tending to my own shit. (Lunch, by the way, at the Bamboo Chopstick was tasty.)

Over the past two decades, demand has escalated for a viable, inoffensive method to transport an individual's fecal matter down from a snowy mountaintop, back to a trailhead, or off an island beach. And lo, inventive minds have been quietly at work, offering aid to the solitary poop packer. We have come a long way with containers, attitudes, and stoutness of hearts. But because I suspect we're not yet at the peak of our genius, reprinted here is the initial discussion of container specifics. Future enhancements of products will be posted on my website.

A user-friendly solo system has to cover much the same territory as the group's, but a designer must take into consideration that the average, hands-on poop packer might be more of a thrice-a-year sojourner, soft on flush apparatus and, in the beginning, more fastidious than, say, the full-time river guide who's become thoroughly inured to outdoor doodies . . . er *duties*. To start off, a collection container should be sturdy but lightweight, small enough to be convincingly carried, yet large enough to hold several deposits. It must have a positively reliable seal; no one wants to think about leakage. A shape convenient for direct deposit would be helpful and, when in use, it shouldn't be inclined to tip over. Lovely would be a pressure-release vent, to rule out its blowing up. Inexpensive, naturally, we'd all appreciate. We're talking either a reusable container—something that's a cinch to flush and clean— or a number that's completely biodegradable. (There is no biodegradable plastic bagging—nor double plastic bagging—currently in existence that will completely contain odors. The zip-locking aluminized Mylar bags handle the odor well, but are not biodegradable. Bear in mind that "biodegradable" in the case of plastic bags is an unregulated term with regard to the required percentage of biodegradable elements and also time involved.) Other pluses might be compatibility with RV dumping stations, trailhead vault toilets, or septic tanks—and I'm going to venture to add here: composting stations. Altogether, it's a tricky bill to fill.

Dismissing for the time being any ideas of hauling around your own dung-devouring scarab beetles, birth of an energy-bar-sized solar incinerator, or backcountry propagation of a big brother to the world's already largest carnivorous plant—the giant montane pitcher plant of Borneo—that the BBC recently reported likes to dine on shrew poo, we'll move on, with no further ado, to considering the whens and hows of packing-it-out. The practice is recommended where hole digging is impossible or not ecological—for explorers gamboling into severe weather conditions, where dirt can't be located or where the tent appears the only place to survive (e.g., Junko and Jim); for hikers in high-use areas, in an effort to keep those places sanitary and looking pristine; for sea kayakers and cavers or anyone visiting fragile ecosystems; for all the untidy Himalayan litterbugs; and for rock climbers (those uncouth beasts!). Understandably, rock climbers have a tough time, given the added acrobatics involved in keeping the face of a mountain clean. What can I say? Practice. Select one of the following modes of assistance and hang off the patio tree.

More quick prefaces to this list: Because the various proprietary "magic" powders used with the bagged products need to be activated by liquid, if you're not peeing in the bag, then pour in $1/2$ to 1 ounce of something like water, coffee . . . beer? And don't drop bagged human excretions into vault toilets or septic systems.

Solo Poop Packer Systems

GO Anywhere Toilet Kit (aka **Wag Bag**) **and the Pee-Wee** ■ www.gocleanwaste.com ■ Cleanwaste ■ 290 Arden Drive ■ Belgrade, MT 59714 ■ Phone: 877-520-0999 ■ Email: info@gocleanwaste.com

Cleanwaste's **GO Anywhere Toilet Kit** ($39.95 for 12-pack) is an extremely lightweight system of two biodegradable plastic bags. The larger and more flexible deposit bag is seeded with Poo Powder; the other is a zip-closing bag of tougher grade. Included in each kit are packets of toilet paper and hand sanitizer. The deposit bag is large enough to spread out on the ground and, as my friend Nancy-the-caver says, "not have to worry about aim." Poo Powder is a nontoxic, proprietary blend that includes a "NASA-developed gelling agent"; it has no smell itself, but controls odor, and begins the breakdown of fecal matter. Each deposit bag contains enough powder to gel 32 ounces (1 quart, or 3 to 4 uses), making it multiple use. Additional bulk Poo Powder ($49.95 for 55 scoops; $87.95 for 120 scoops; plus a measuring scoop) will extend the use of a bag. A new item, the Pee-Wee ($114 for 12-pack of 6 bags each; retail prices weren't available yet), is a unisex urine bag with Poo Powder that will gel 24 ounces of liquid. It can be used by adults or children when "plumbing's not available." When finished, snap the collar closed. Toss Cleanwaste's used bags into the regular garbage (okay by EPA guidelines). GO Anywheres are providing a sanitary approach for dozens of activities—hiking, boating, cycling, hunting, horse packing—as well as for the military, long-haul truckers, hospitals, and FEMA.

With the GO Anywheres in such wide use, they rate further discussion, particularly for backpackers. Joshua Cole, Outward Bound program director in Washington State, tells his students, "Don't tie the bag on the outside of your pack, where it can get poked by a branch or pecked by a bird." A group of his had cached their GO Anywheres in the snow while they took a day hike, and they returned to camp only to find "a murder of crows" upon them. Cole recommends tucking a laden bag inside the top of your pack, where it won't get squashed by the load, and then definitely remembering when you take a break not to sit on that corner. Bags will pop by force, he says, but if you're careful, they work "really well."

RESTOP 2, RESTOP 1, RESTOP 2W ■ www.restop.com ■ American Innotek, Inc. ■ 2320 Meyers Avenue ■ Escondido, CA 92029 ■ Toll free: 800-366-3941; or 760-741-6600 ■ Email: info@whennaturecalls.com

The **RESTOP 2** ($3 each; $30 for 10-pack; $300 for 100-pack) is a patented "bag-within-a-bag" system that's seeded with a proprietary polymer/enzyme blend that biodegrades, gels, and deodorizes human waste. Each kit comes with toilet paper and an antiseptic toilette. The zip-locking transport bag is made of gas-impervious, 3-mil aluminized Mylar, for containing odor. Attached is a gray amply-sized plastic bag with a bottom that opens into the transport bag. Use with a commode or spread it directly on the ground. After you've made your deposit, pick up the plastic portion and cinch it closed with the black plastic drawstring—this motion serves to slide your deposit on down into the silvery bag where the floral smelling powder blend resides—then roll the plastic portion back into the transport bag, and zip closed. Though it's meant to be a one-use bag, there's enough powder to process "more waste than you could possibly cram in the bag"—reportedly 4 to 5 uses. Used RESTOP bags are "landfill-friendly" (in line with EPA guidelines) and can be tossed into the regular trash. The RESTOP 1 ($4 for a 2-pack; $8 for a 4-pack) is a disposable unisex urine bag equipped with a one-way valve to prevent spillage, a plastic collar with a pop-open tab that becomes a handle, and enough proprietary blend to gel 20 ounces of pee. The RESTOP 2W ($15) is a Wilderness Waste Containment Pouch and a 5-pack of RESTOP 2s. The Pouch is a lightweight tote bag of tough plastic mesh for carrying out used bags.

Biffy Bag ■ **www.biffybag.com** ■ LEDO Environmental, LLC ■ 3951 North View Lane ■ Woodbury, MN 55125 ■ Phone: 651-206-3078 ■ Email: info@biffybag.com

The **Biffy Bag**—also called the "pocket potty" or "biffy in a jiffy"—($3.49 each; $9.99 for 3-pack; $31.99 for 10-pack; also sold in quantities of 25 and 100) is another two-bag system, but with some decided differences. The outer zip-locking transport bag is made of gas-impervious, aluminized Mylar for odor control. The inner biodegradable green plastic bag has a narrowed, rounded bottom that facilitates bringing the treatment powder directly into contact with the deposit (with everything ending up inside the plastic bag, inside the gas-impervious bag—or actually double-bagged.) The proprietary Biffy Powder actively foams up around the deposit, immediately placing a sealing layer on the top, while engulfing and neutralizing waste and odors (with enzymes and a decay catalyst), and then it solidifies from the top down. Comes with a packet of Biffy Powder, toilet paper, and an oversized hand-wipe. Designed for one use (for sanitary purposes) but reports have it that bags have been employed for as many as four poops. Contains enough enzymes and decay catalyst to take care of four, but to ensure complete solidification you might want to order more Biffy Powder ($4.99 for 4-pack). When ready, open the silvery bag, grab the inner green bag, and add the Biffy Powder. Next, tear the two tabs along their perforations—turning them into straps that tie around your waist—and clamp the bag onto your, so to speak, poop deck. Then, reach between your legs, pull the bag-front forward, bend your knees slightly, and go for it. It can also be used with a commode, if you prefer a seat. Used Biffy Bags conform to EPA guidelines; drop them in the trash.

Though there is no standardized testing, this outfit touts a burst-strength rating of 50 psi and a puncture-resistance rating of 13 psi and 4,000 times the odor containment of a typical garbage bag. A loaded Biffy Bag survived a 20-foot drop onto pavement, intact.

Double Doodie Waste Bags ■ Reliance Products ■ 1093 Sherwin Road ■ Winnipeg, Manitoba ■ R3H 1A4 Canada ■ Phone (for wholesale orders): 800-665-0258

Reliance's **Double Doodie Bag** ($14.99 or less for 6-pack) is another double-bagging system, this time with proprietary Bio-Gel. You can purchase the bags with or without the Bio-Gel, so check what you're getting. (Double Doodie Plus Bags always come with Bio-Gel.) Use in a campground with one of the Reliance commodes (see page 51), or in the backcountry directly on the ground. Provide your own toilet paper and hand-washing arrangement.

Clean Mountain Can ∎ GTS, Inc. ∎ 4037 East English Street ∎
Wichita, KS 67218 ∎ Phone: 785-505-1482 ∎ Email: pabecker@aol.com

GTS's **Clean Mountain Can** ($69.95) is a straight-sided barrel
(8$\frac{1}{2}$-inch diameter x 10$\frac{3}{4}$-inch height) made of high-density polyethylene, sturdy enough for sitting upon. It's equipped with an
8-inch-diameter hole, a screw-type lid, and a Gortex gas-release
vent. Included is a webbing harness for locking down its lid and
strapping it onto a pack, sled, or, presumably, a mule. Dry weight
is 1.65 pounds and capacity 18 to 20 user-days. CMCs were used
on the Eco Everest Expedition. And Kiliwarriors, a small Maa-
sai outfitter for Kilimanjaro climbs, has been valiantly removing
excrement in CMCs from the overnight Crater Camp since 2004—
although theirs is pretty much a lone struggle. Alaska's Denali
Climbing Rangers endorse CMCs. Removal of human waste from
Denali's high camp at 17,200 feet has been required since 2006.
The National Park Service (NPS) purchased 1,100 CMCs for cir-
culation and arranged for a dumping and cleaning service. The
system is funded, in part, by climber fees. A privately owned CMC
may be dumped at a sewage treatment plant or an RV dumping
station. Then wash the can at home with soap and water and a
designated brush. Hint: Lining the can with a GO Anywhere bag
and adding more Poo Powder cuts down on cleanup, but then be
sure to toss the bag in the garbage. NPS's website (www.nps.gov/
dena/planyourvisit/cmc.htm) contains all the CMC information,
and GTS sells them wholesale or retail.

Big Wall Can ∎ www.mtntools.com/can/bigwall ∎ Mountain Tools ∎
P.O. Box 222295 ∎ Carmel, CA 93922 ∎ Phone: 800-510-2514/
for tech questions: 831-620-0911 ∎ Email: On the website, click on
"ask the tool man"

Mountain Tools' **Big Wall Can** ($69.95) is the Clean Mountain
Can with a different webbing harness, for hauling. Stacks right
under a haul bag. "Because nature doesn't necessarily schedule
her calls for convenient locations"—that is, it's not so easy to sit
on a swinging can—extreme climbers do their number twos in

a brown paper bag, then roll it up and tuck it into the can. Pre-rigging the paper bags with a bit of kitty litter is recommended. A BWC's contents can be dumped at pit toilets or RV dumping stations. Mountain Tools will ship anywhere, including to General Delivery (say, at Yosemite) to accommodate traveling climbers.

Shhh-it! Kit ■ **www.KathleenintheWoods.net** ■ P.O. Box 342 ■ Victor, MT 59875 ■ Email: kit@KathleenintheWoods.net

The **Shhh-it! Kit** ($29.95) is a washable, reusable personal container designed for the backpacker, sea kayaker, canoeist, long-distance cyclist, cross-country skier . . . even the 4-wheeler and big game hunter. The lightweight aluminum cylinder of 3-inch diameter x 12 inches long (or custom cut to any length your heart desires—and signed, if you want!), is equipped with rubber-gasketed screw-on lids at both ends. The 12-inch Sojouner weighs.62 pounds and holds 3 to 4 deposits with corresponding t.p. (depending, of course, on a person's intake—do you eat like a butterfly, a pink flamingo, or a wild boar?—and the amount of tissue required). The 9-inch Sprinter, for shorter trips, accommodates 2 to 3 poops. No pressure-release vent, but during testing, a packed tube, under two days of direct California sun, never blew a lid. The Shhh-it! Kit can be tucked inside a backpack, along with supplies of t.p., paper wraps, and hand sanitizer, or into the special SK Ditty Bag ($10.00) and strapped to the outside, where it can take the air. Deposits are made simply, and almost anywhere, onto a couple squares of absorbent paper (unbleached paper tow-eling is recommended, but make certain it's the kind that holds together when wet—test first at home with water). Now, the next step is where things can veer toward creative: Yep, wrap up your leaving like a burrito and slip it into the cylinder. In seriously wet or snowy conditions, for insurance, spread out a piece of wax paper first. Paper wrappings are biodegradable and they're also helpful when it comes to post-trip cleaning. With the Shhh-it! Kit there are no plastic bags to worry about perforating or plugging up the honey wagon's pump, no poo powder to spill, no smell, no flies. Empty the cylinder into any pit- or vault-type toilet, those found in national parks, campgrounds, take-outs, and trailheads. To push your packages on through, remove both lids. Carry some sort of utensil in your vehicle, stored in a plastic bag: for instance, a long-handled kitchen spoon or spatula (not wooden), bent with pliers to handy angles. I use a whisk! Unless you've been stricken with traveler's trots, your burritos generally are tidy little packages that pop right out. Clean with a bottle brush reserved solely for this purpose and keep it stashed perhaps alongside your home toilet bowl brush. After thoroughly washing with soap and water, and disinfectant if you wish (no lousy threads on the inside to make life difficult), leave the tool and cylinder in your vehicle. The Shhh-it! Kit, granted, will not be the best system for everyone. Lightweight, streamlined, and durable, it's the option for the extra brave and adventurous, and those wanting to go no-frills, inexpensive, and reusable.

Do-It-Yourself Poop Tubes

The first **Poop Tube** (about $15 for parts, without glue) arrived on the scene more than sixteen years ago in the high Sierras, via Mark Butler, an NPS physical science specialist and climber. Although he made no claims on the tube's design, he used one, promoted them as inexpensive make-at-home containers for packing-it-out, and advocated their use on the climbing routes in Yosemite National Park. Voilà! An end to flinging laden paper bags into thin air. Construction is easy and materials available in hardware or plumbing stores. Simply cut a piece of white PVC pipe (4-inch diameter) to the length of your trip, so to speak, or 10 to 20 inches. Glue a cap on one end and a slip/thread coupling for a screw plug on the other (see illustration). A 12-inch tube weighs 2.3 pounds. With super tape (climber's webbing) and a little duct tape, sling the tube from the bottom of your haul sack. Deposits are made into brown paper bags seeded with kitty litter, and then stuffed into the tube. At the end of the trip, the contents are dumped into a pit or vault toilet.

A variant is made out of black ABS pipe. The instructions are on the Internet (www.blm.gov/or/resources/recreation/rogue/portable-toilets-kayak.php). Personally, I'd go with the PVC solely because of the color; it won't cook its contents the way black does.

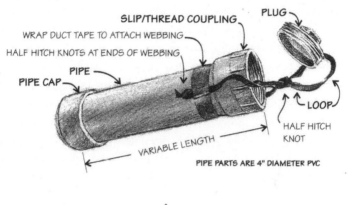

SLIP/THREAD COUPLING
PLUG
WRAP DUCT TAPE TO ATTACH WEBBING
HALF HITCH KNOTS AT ENDS OF WEBBING
PIPE
PIPE CAP
LOOP
HALF HITCH KNOT
VARIABLE LENGTH
PIPE PARTS ARE 4" DIAMETER PVC

For the average adventurer, who's willing to leave behind Western civilization's characteristic prudishness, there are more home-grown ways of coping, and I don't mean enemas or the untraceable rumor of biodegradable bags made of cheese. Inexpensive household containers have been appropriated for outdoor use on many occasions. I have reports of plastic snap-lid salad bowls servicing backpackers, two people to a bowl in some cases. (I couldn't help wondering whether this type of sharing cements relationships in the same way that showering together during a drought does.) One flaw in the system involves methane buildup: a morning's hike under a hot sun will invariably pop the seal. But people seem to manage by being attentive. Karen Stimpson, as trail keeper for the Maine Island Trail, once revealed that a bowl of similar design was her favorite. She started out with the kitty litter routine, but progressed to rolling her deposit in a bit of sand, earth, or dried leaves before scooping it up. "The container cleans easier," she said. Surely this is all new testimony to the function of salad bowls. One note on kitty litter: buy the cheapest available, as it's usually straight bentonite, a powdery clay soil.

If you lack expertise with gravity, like me, here are a few hints on solitary collecting in a snowscape. Scoop out a small depression and tuck your container into it. With the leisure and inclination, you can build a throne, a chair-high mound with a container hole in the seat. Too cold to plunk right down? Carefully, rest your buns upon your gloves.

Completely from another realm, in the last decade of the twentieth century, came another form of backcountry human waste disposal. Called, in different parts of the country, "smearing" and "frosting a rock," the activity became cause for a great deal of mirth in this book's second edition. I wrote: "A hiker rises from an afternoon nap, takes in a panoramic sweep of mountain pinnacles, languidly stretches, then proclaims to all present, 'I think I'll go frost a rock.'" There were those onlookers who weren't altogether sure that child's play hadn't sparked the cranial gears of some cruiser through rugged terrain. No one ever owned up! Now after almost two decades, the prevailing thinking about this type of disposal has changed, and for a number of good reasons. (I'm guessing your imagination will carry you through this discussion to where I provide better illumination.)

Beyond the obvious—that most anywhere that human excrement is left exposed, insects and animals are readily drawn to it—we now know from the conclusions of pertinent field studies that microorganisms in fecal smears, even under circumstances of close to optimal conditions and technique, can persist a lot longer than originally assumed. As can the feces themselves. Together, the Leave No Trace Center for Outdoor Ethics, the National Park Service, Ferris State University, and the National Outdoor Leadership School undertook a series of studies on the fate of feces and fecal microorganisms contained in samples of varying thickness, in three different environments—arid and temperate and alpine. Sites were picked in Mount Rainier National Park and the Wenatchee National Forest. The principle investigator was Michael D. Ells (copies of the studies and photos are available from the LNT Center for Outdoor Ethics: 800-332-4100 or info@lnt.org).

Someone obviously offered up a lovely specimen and others donned protective gloves. At the arid and temperate sites, smears were set up inside wire cages, for keeping out animals; and then, at all sites, elaborate monitoring took place over a period of months, with varied results. Insects at one location arrived within 15 minutes and insect larvae at another was evident on day two; smears at some locations began to desiccate in short order; but fecal organisms at other sites were found surviving at four-and-a-half months. Because the testing was limited to fecal *bacteria*, the staying power of such items as viruses, protozoa, and helminthes (or worms) was not included. Many questions arose. Further testing was a suggestion.

Coupling the findings of these studies with wider casual observations of wilderness smears brings to the fore this axiom: Optimal smearing is not something often accomplished. Humans, come to find out, aren't terribly talented at fecal artistry. *Some* of us were instead—chickening out?—leaving plain piles in the open or whipping up lumpy mashed-potatolike toppings, rather than painstakingly smushing our crap to the required paper-thin veneer. Ultimately, at the top of considerations must reside our cherished wildlife and waterways, as well as others of our own species, all of whom/which stand vulnerable to raw human feces. Thus, the very outdoor schools that first adopted smearing are no longer promoting it. And I'm not promoting it. Packing-it-out is superior in all but extremely select situations, while also being— for those of us who've aged gracefully beyond our uninhibited years of preschool and finger-painting—a heck of a lot easier (or hard enough) to get the hang of. Yet, I will describe the method here and offer the severe cautions, as it's foolish to ignore the whole topic in the hope that someone who barely grasps its outline is not out roaming the mountains, experimenting.

Frosting, alas, is not a matter for the timid or the tyro. Much is required of you to execute a smear in a proper and safe fashion: first and foremost, a personal predilection for elbowing straight to the head of sticky situations; second, a well-schooled background in meteorology, climate, and terrain; and third, a finely honed sense of aesthetics. What follows is solely this author's recommendation for an activity that, until we know more, should be an absolute rarity. Four elements MUST be present: an extremely remote location, intense sunlight, a dry landscape, and scant soil (that is, no bacterial activity or limited soil depth). This presumes your travel is above timberline or nearly so, through blazing deserts, or across extensive boulder fields. If you're not traversing a dry climate, it must be a long, dry season with no chance of fecal matter being carried away by storm runoff or buried beneath snowdrifts to thaw in the spring. Remoteness is a huge criteria. It's not cricket to ruin the next person's well-deserved sojourn through scenic grandeur. If an area is likely to receive visitors (let's go for an outside margin) within 6 months of your passing, you should be packing-it-out, not smearing. In effect, you are employing the sewage treatment plant of the heavens, the almighty solar incinerator: ultraviolet rays scorch the life out of pathogens and dehydrate your leavings until the wind carries off the final parched flakes.

This brings us to actual procedure. With sunbeams the prime factor in desiccation, select a spot that catches daylong direct rays. Your spatula will be a handy stone. First, you shit on the rock. Then go ahead and frost away, as thinly as possible, leaving the stone alongside, also turned up to the sun. When, long ago, I'd asked, "Just how thin are we talking here?" the answer came "Pretend you're frosting a cake." But as it turns out, even that's a bit too thick; think of it more as rolling out paint onto a wall. If midway into your plastering, you start to come a little unstuck, don't UNDER ANY CIRCUMSTANCES give up and go home. Shift your vision, perhaps to picturing it as another miracle in the long list given us by the sun gods, Helios and Apollo.

🌱

Our wild lands shrink. Our urban lifestyles manufacture more madness. Our longing to touch nature increases. More high use of cherished lands is directly ahead. Simple arithmetic tells us that fewer one-sit holes and more packing-it-out will expand the limits of visitation. In essence, a ballooning backcountry population and a disappearing wilderness translate into more crap in your pack! Something to remember next time your vote is needed for wildland preservation.

So off we go, wending Earth's curves from her craggy rock faces to her seashore marshes, and all in the company of jolly good friends, with only one act likely remaining solitary—that of shitting. But take comfort in the thought that you won't, in fact, be alone—in either the queasiness or the shared virtue. Trust me, individual porta looing is becoming a backwoods tsunami. Don't be a laggard. Grab your container. Bring your clothespin, if it helps. And take those little piles with you when you leave.

McVey '89

5 Trekker's Trots

Lomotil, Lomotil, wherefore art thou, my Lomotil?
  —Anonymous traveler in Puerto Vallarta

During the violent shaking of an earthquake, a solid, earth-filled dam can turn into liquid and wash away. Trekker's trots is a similar phenomenon occurring within the intestinal walls of the mammalian body. I've seen it happen to my Clydesdales during Fourth of July fireworks at the county fair. Seconds after the first cannon blasts, the horses are dispersing streams of green alfalfa soup. When this instantaneous liquefaction happens in the species *Homo sapiens*, we call it *turista, trekker's trots, Montezuma's revenge, the green-apple two-step*, or, quite simply, *the shits*.

Such a watery biological response can be brought about by any number of things in addition to flus and intestinal diseases. Our immune systems grow up where we do, leaving our resistance unequipped for various foreign foods and water. Traveling itself can be overwhelming; changes in climate, altitude, and time zone all take their toll on the human system. Anxiety about making all (or missing half) your travel connections can have anyone reaching for the Riopan Plus or Kaopectate. Or the sheer fright of an adventure a bit too thrilling can "set it off" faster than a shaken beer exits its bottle. Two of my favorite friends seem to be hit by this particular disorder whenever they set foot inside an airport; thus, they've coined another modern euphemism, *airporters*, for that most dreaded of afflictions.

This short chapter—short, as I hope all your bouts with this subject will be—emphasizes prevention. Once you've been struck by an airporter, there isn't a whole lot to be said—only to resist cleaning up in a nearby creek and remember to do any washing above the high-water line. It helps to have a trusted friend (maybe someone named Jim), to bring you wash water and clothes and offer comfort. Someone who won't hold her sides in uproarious laughter.

Focusing on prevention automatically brings us face to face with sanitation practices. Because enteric pathogens (the intestinal bad guys) are transmitted by forms of fecal-oral contact, logically, then, the first step toward prevention is to ritualize hand washing. Get yourself and all your traveling companions into the habit of washing *after* squatting and *before* preparing food or eating. Be neurotic about it! The importance of hand washing can't be stressed enough for outdoor people who tend to equate ruggedness—that messing and sweating about in earth's fresh fragrant dirt—with the *primeval*, the long-sought-after excuse not to bathe for days. Near the camp loo on a commercial river trip, the guides will station biodegradable soap and a spigoted water container or a bucket of water with a long-handled ladle. Use it!

An imaginative setup for the private trip is the *refried bean wash*, concocted by my cohort in the study of backcountry fecal management, Dan Ritzman. The idea sprang from traditional camp fare: Rosarita refried beans, chili and beans, pork and beans, bean pot stew—there's always a bean can around. The larger the can, the longer the wash. Punch two holes opposite each other near the top rim of an empty, cleaned can and tie a string or wire between them to make a pail-like handle. Punch a third hole in the can's side near the bottom. Fill with fresh water and the bottom hole will produce a steady stream for soaping and rinsing. Dan sets it at the front edge of a flat-topped boulder or hangs it in a tree. Nowadays, hydration bags or reservoirs, with shut-off clamps on the hose, will do the same job.

Another precaution against traveler's diarrhea entails watching closely what you eat and drink. Properly refrigerate perishable foods and carefully disinfect all water for drinking, cooking, dishwashing, and food washing. Other guidebooks extensively cover food matters; here, I address the off-road issue of *field water disinfection*, or treatment of wilderness water for infectious organisms. In view of today's far-reaching Internet access, as well as rapid changes in product lines, and the convenience of comparison printouts available at outdoor stores (and "gear reviews" at www. trailspace.com), what follows is a general discussion rather than extensive reviews of apparatus. With this overview, you'll have a head start on the dizzying array of disinfecting processes available today. Seeking deeper information? Hook up with Paul S. Auerbach's *Wilderness Medicine* (St. Louis: C. V. Mosby Company; 5th edition, 2007, 2,336 pages) for more than you'll probably want or need on everything—from splints and slings to which way to jump when a volcano erupts. Sells for $209, but you can flip through a copy at your local medical library. The reason I mention it here is for its intensely researched forty-odd pages on field water treatment, including critiques of methods and apparatus, all written by Dr. Howard Backer, M.D., who has for roughly a quarter century held the position of "genius and authority" on the subject.

First let's clear up a few terms. According to Dr. Backer, who's also an avid outdoorsman, *disinfection* means "removing or destroying harmful microorganisms," and should not be confused with *sterilization*, "the destruction or removal of all life forms," which is "not necessary, since not all organisms are enteric human pathogens." This is not to say that those processes that do kill everything are to be ignored. *Purification* is a term that also shows up in products' promotional literature. Backer calls it, technically, "the removal of organic or inorganic chemicals and particulate matter, including radioactive particles." Although "purification can eliminate offensive color, taste, and odor, it may not remove or kill microorganisms." That said, there are some "purification" systems that do what they claim to do.

Categories are next. Enteric pathogens come in three, listed here in descending size: parasitic organisms, bacteria, and viruses (P, B, and V). In the first are the protozoan cysts of *Giardia* and the oocysts of *Cryptosporidium* and, as discussed in chapter 2, they are widespread in wilderness water and must be considered a potential hazard everywhere in the world. Bacteria that are problematic cannot be called epidemic in the backcountry of either the U.S. or Canada, but *E. coli* and *Salmonella* do turn up and are seemingly on the increase. If you're traveling to developing countries where sanitation is poor and municipal water supplies (even hotel tap water) are suspect, you'll need further protection from waterborne viruses, such as cholera and hepatitis A.

Any number of mechanical filtration systems—some hand pumps, some sip bottles, some gravity feeds for larger groups and base camps—will effectively remove protozoan cysts. To varying degrees, the same systems block bacteria. A filter with an "absolute" pore size of 3.0 microns will remove *Giardia* and *Cryptosporidium*; a filter of 0.2 microns will eliminate all bacteria ("absolute" means that no organism bigger than that size can pass through). Although the Environmental Protection Agency doesn't "approve" or "endorse" field water filtration units, as such, they do offer guidelines, and many products conform to these. Products sporting an EPA registration number have merely been registered as a pesticide (as in iodine) and tested and found not to cause "harmful health effects."

Filters do their job by trapping microorganisms in their elements or cartridges that are made of various materials, including ceramic, silica, pleated glass fibers, and hollow plastic fibers, all of which can strain out protozoa and bacteria. A pump with a chemical-free, structured matrix (unique to First Need Products) removes protozoa, bacteria, *and* viruses. But more on viruses later.

Both the life of a filter (usually given in gallon capacity) and the system's flow rate (how fast you can fill your water bottle) will drastically fluctuate downward when you're pumping muddy, debris-laden, or glacial water; when your apparatus is partially clogged; or when Sasquatch plants a big foot on your hose. Prefilters are for capturing the larger crud and sediment. You can also prefilter the prefilter by using cheesecloth, a bandana, or a coffee filter, or by letting the water sit for a while to settle out. Some pumps are designed to back-flush to unclog the filter; others are cleaned by scrubbing the filter's outer surface; still others can't be cleaned at all. With any filter, examine the housing regularly for cracks that might admit contamination. And become familiar with the cost of replacement filters, because eventually they all need to be changed. The ceramic filters are initially expensive but last the longest and are cleaned easily with a brush. Activated carbon filters, which come integrated with other filters or as add-ons,

will helpfully remove organic chemicals such as herbicides, pes-
ticides, diesel fuel, solvents, and fertilizers, as well as the iodine
you might have used to kill viruses. On the downside, carbon filters require frequent replacement, regardless of whether they are
clogged. They collect material by the process of *adsorption* (the
clinging of molecules to a solid surface), and when surface limits
are reached, previously adsorbed materials begin to dislodge. On
the other hand, some companies claim their cartridges will clog
long before the capacity of the activated carbon is used up.

It's an advantage to have a pump that handily dismantles for
cleaning and field maintenance (don't forget to carry parts and
tools). Some models demand the skill of an arthroscopic surgeon;
ask for a demonstration. Keep in mind that the perfect filter does
not exist—there are always trade-offs—and no filter will give you
100 percent protection. Other things to consider are price, weight,
durability, flow rate, ease in pumping, adequate length in hoses,
your group size, and the duration of your trip. Let's not forget
accessories: lid adapters for direct pumping into your favorite trail
bottle; tote bags; and, in some cases, the prefilter and carbon filter.

Now for those deadly little guys, viruses, and a look at several
applications that, when properly executed, are capable of eliminating P, B, and V in one fell swoop. A mechanical filtration system with a pore size fine enough to strain out viruses will make
driving water through it impossible. (In general, the smaller the
pore size, the harder the pumping.) So, to knock out viruses, we
turn elsewhere.

Boiling is the tried-and-true method from early days, when
people were few and firewood was plentiful, and it's always an
option for killing all waterborne enteric pathogens, immediately.
From Dr. Backer again: ". . . any water is adequately disinfected
by the time it reaches the boiling point [let's call it a rolling boil]—
even at altitudes of 24,000 feet where the boiling point is as low
as 74.5°C." But the CDC, EPA, and others, according to Backer,
recommend a 1-minute boil for added safety, and at higher eleva-
tions, make that 3 minutes. The major drawback—in our age of

Leave No Trace Ethics and not wanting to break branches off all the trees bordering a campsite—is in dragging around enough fuel to accomplish the job.

Ultraviolet light in a gadget of a size manageable for backpackers is a fairly new offering. Actually more than manageable: the miracle wands, about the size of a small bottle of Elmer's glue and powered by smaller batteries, will *sterilize* large quantities of water in almost a flash. They are, however, delicate, useless on murky water, and finicky in freezing temperatures. If you spring for one, treat it gingerly and plan time for prewarming it in your armpit and for prefiltering silt and floaties. One model boasts a cool solar battery recharger you can rig to ride atop your pack.

The **MIOX Purifier** is a system of salt tablets that electrolytically change into a chloroxygen chemical compound. The MIOX comes with a mixing container the size of a highlighting marker, and batteries and test strips. Good for treating large volumes of water and it's maintenance free. Will inactivate B and V and (with enough time) P. Be sure to read the hazards.

General Ecology's First Need Delux Portable Water Purifier is a double-action pump with a proprietary "structured matrix filter" that incorporates charcoal. It removes chemicals and P, B, and V without use of halogens (see below). Produces 1.8 quarts per minute, with a capacity of 125 gallons. Cannot be cleaned, and must be replaced. Rates high on test results.

Halogens are the chemical disinfectants **chlorine** and **iodine**. Chlorine has long been the preferred disinfectant for municipal water supplies and iodine has been used by the military since the beginning of the 1900s. Although halogens work well on V and B, P organisms have a resistance to them. *Cryptosporidium*, in particular, is highly resistant to chlorine. Plan on waiting the allotted time—3 minutes to 4 hours or more—or additionally filter mechanically for protozoa before (or after) halogenating. Halogens will not disinfect adequately when prepared in insufficient concentrations or without allowing adequate contact time. High pH, colder water temperatures, and cloudy water all decrease effectiveness.

Chlorine-dioxide tablets are safer to use than household liquid bleach. Iodine is available in tablets, crystals, and tincture.

Because the stability of tablets is sometimes questionable and they are inexpensive, always buy a new bottle before each trip and keep it tightly sealed and out of the heat. You must be mindful of the corrosive effects of halogens, particularly of carelessly handled iodine crystals.

Finally, when you have beautifully disinfected your water with halogens, the result is the not-so-lovely chemical taste. Because less halogen means better taste, you can improve on it in several ways: prefilter cloudy water, use warmer water, or allow for a longer contact time. Some people seem to adapt readily to drinking iodine water, happily disguising it with lemonade powder or Tang. I always think they have flavor-impaired taste buds. But iodine is only an odor, sensed in the nose and not on the tongue. When you run out of instant cherry drink, try pinching your nose. Or see Potable Aqua Plus below.

The following products are iodine based. **Polar Pure** is a bottle of iodine crystals with a neat little trap to safely contain them. A thermometer on the side of the bottle tells you what the dosage should be. The crystals are long lasting and not affected by age or exposure to air.

Potable Aqua comes as a wee bottle of 50 iodine tablets. One tablet will treat a quart of water in 3 minutes. If the water is turbid or extremely cold it takes two tablets and 20 minutes. Bring a magnifying glass to read the instructions.

Potable Aqua Plus is Potable Aqua with an additional bottle of iodine neutralizer tablets, for a two-step application. The Plus converts iodine into a flavorless, odorless iodide. The active ingredient in the chemical change is ascorbic acid, or vitamin C.

Use of **iodine** warrants a few medical warnings: **do not take when pregnant, or if you have iodine sensitivity or a history** (even *family* history) **of thyroid disease**.

In the end, choose a system that fits your lifestyle and suits the places you plan to visit. Are you an avid day hiker, or a mountain peak to pinnacle nut? Are you organizing the Stamp Collectors Club for a weekend excursion, or off to the Amazon in a dugout? Safe drinking water is serious business. Approach with caution any products ringing of fads or resembling toys. Read the fine print, ask questions, feel satisfied. In Montana, I found the outdoor folks working in the local outfitting establishments well versed in equipment and over the top in friendliness and helpfulness.

🌿

On trips to Mexico in the 1960s, I clutched my prescription bottle of tiny Lomotil tablets with the preoccupation of a small child with a death grip on her teddy bear. In those days, Lomotil was all that a general practitioner knew to recommend. These days, you can buy Imodium over-the-counter and travel medicine has become a specialty, called *emporiatrics*. A network of travel clinics strung around the country offers informational handouts, provides pre-trip immunizations, suggests appropriate prophylactic medications, and diagnoses post-trip ailments (most people will be home by the time *Giardia* symptoms first appear).

Prophylactic drugs for a mild case of *turista* are generally not advised for healthy travelers because the medication can get in the way of diagnosis and treatment if you contract something more serious. The exception to this is Pepto-Bismol, which is both a light preventive and a cure. Consult your health care provider prior to foreign travel about using Pepto-Bismol.

If, after all this, trekker's trots happens to get you, it's critical to maintain your hydration. Oral hydration can usually be accomplished with glasses of water and those little packets from the World Health Organization or your local health food store, as long as you, of course, remember to pack them. Otherwise, drink alternate 8-ounce glasses of:

1. Orange, apple, or any fruit juice rich in potassium with a teaspoon of honey and a pinch of salt. (For me, the taste of salt in fruit juice triggers an automatic gag reflex; instead, I fall back on the old tequila routine—lick the salt from my hand, chug the juice.)
2. Water, with a teaspoon of baking soda as a buffer for stomach acid.

If nothing else, down some salt and a Coke. Diarrhea combined with vomiting can create a life-threatening loss of body fluid. If you can't keep down rehydration drinks—particularly in a hot climate—seek medical attention and intravenous fluids.

While we're on the subject of *remembering*, wash your hands! Particularly after cleaning your diseased filtration pump. And don't stuff midday traveler's snacks into your mouth with grubby paws. I'm a great one for riding second-class buses, running my hands over railings and seat backs and window frames, then at some stop buying a treat from a street vendor—the deliciousness of which is to eat with my fingers while loitering.

Abide by good advice and you can avoid most cases of traveler's trots, as long as you don't stumble out of the jungle into a colorful roadside café, delirious, and order a bottle of warm pop dumped over contaminated ice cubes.

6 For Women Only: How Not to Pee in Your Boots

The significance of my position was the opportunity for my growth.
　—Valerie Fons, *Keep It Moving*

A chapter for women. Why not? I've been a female all my life, as many a pair of soggy socks, jaundiced sneakers, and rancid leather boots can attest. Men need no pointers on how to pee. Men can pee and maintain the decorum of a three-piece-suiter strolling down Park Avenue. To whizz, men just find a tree. Not to hide behind, thank you, but to lean on while pondering the goings-on of the universe—one hand propped high on the trunk, the other aiming penis. With backs turned but in full view of the world, men piss for anyone present, sometimes in baronial silhouette against a blazing sunset, sometimes without a break in the conversation, as if the flaunting of their ritual were the greater part of its pleasure. Women, on the other hand, search for a place to hide (heaven forbid anyone should know we have to pee in the first place), where, with panties dropped and sweet asses bared, we must assume the position of a flustered duck trying to watch itself pass an egg.

Possibly Freud deserves more credit than I normally grant him. Although I don't recall a childhood Oedipal complex, in adulthood there have been occasions when, along with the urge to pee, I've been seized by a fierce penis envy. As a rule, men pee with dignity, it might even be said with class—sometimes with machismo alone, but always with ease. Except when troubled by inclement conditions reflected in the time-honored proverb, "Never into the wind," men, by and large, are carefree pee-ers. It's high time women peed with a similar sense of pride and had as much fun.

So cheer up, my dears, the rest of this chapter is just for us. With a little practice we, too, can cultivate the ultimate in blasé, while being proud of a challenge faced and won, a job well done. (Not just a piddling vaingloriousness in the operation of an appendage come by genetically!)

Had I paid more attention when I was growing up in the forties and fifties, my grandmother might well have been my illustrious peeing mentor. Now I have only the remembrance of accompanying her into public restrooms. Hoisting her skirts, she would slip one leg out of her wide-legged underdrawers, twist them around the other leg to hold outstretched matador-fashion, and then with the shuffle of a too tightly reined horse, back bowlegged over the bowl and fire away. In those days, I had no time for this bizarre old-fashioned method: I was too busy balancing little bits of folded toilet paper all around the seat (as my mother had taught me), half of which ended upon on the floor from the slight breeze caused by my turning around to sit down. Finding with regularity that a person could water her pants before successfully executing this preparation, I eventually gave it up and just sat down. It was my perhaps ignorant but expedient theory that if everyone else were following this ridiculous paper routine, the seat must surely be free from whatever frightful diseases were to be avoided— diseases never explained, only alluded to mysteriously.

To this day, except where sanitary seat tissues ("butt gaskets" in some circles) are furnished for resting upon, I have yet to master a reliable restroom technique. Sometimes I try bracing myself against the stall's walls, toilet tank, or paper dispenser, or even hanging on to the doorknob (if there is one), in an effort to suspend my bum an inch above the seat. About then I remember a couple of friends: one who lets herself in and out of cubicles and flushes public toilets with her shoe rather than come in skin contact with those germ-ridden levers; the other, a man, who choreographs an elaborate routine for escaping the men's room without touching a thing. Unnerving me further while seated on a sanitary cover is this idle question: if the last person's pee can soak through this thin tissue shield, what else might there be swimming through? Oh, grandmother and baggy underwear, where are you now?

Fortunately, out in the bush we face none of these civilized problems. Give me peeing in the woods any day. Once you get the hang of it, it's a blissful experience. After a long outdoor stint, I find I'm severely depressed with the cold, white, closed-in ambiance and flushing racket of my home bathroom.

In developing countries, another stand-up peeing style (outshining even my grandmother's) is performed by women who grow up unhampered by trousers. The secret lies somewhere in the gathering up of a skirt, the tilting of a pelvis, and the near bowing of femurs— plus, the sometimes-suggested placement of your first two fingers on either side of the inner labia, to gently position your stream outward—which altogether allow for peeing with Olympian accuracy. All made easier by practice since toddler age. And yet . . . I recently met a United Nations representative in arts and education who fairly boasted she'd learned her stand-up peeing at the age of forty-five, from the Asante women of Ghana.

Today women think of skirts as less than functional in the woods. The fact that men were originally assigned pants and women skirts was due, in all probability, not to high fashion but to sheer biological practicality. If you should so desire, don't hesitate to scramble the outbacks in a dirndl or sarong, as did Robyn Davidson, the author of *Tracks* (New York: Pantheon Books, 1980), when crossing the Australian desert with her camels. "Whatever works" is a good philosophy. When we pass on the trail, I'll recognize another independent, experimental spirit. Who can tell? Someday our inhibitions about crotch exposure might evaporate in a rebellion similar to "ban the bra," bringing us full circle to a resurrection of the bare-bottomed leopard-skin mini! For practical reasons.

I've always said someone could make a fortune designing pants for women with a comfortable Velcro-closing crotch. The original designer and proprietor of Zanika Sportswear, Vicki Morgan, will surely go down in history. Morgan's company, recently bought by Janice L. Anderson, is now called **The Outdoor Woman**. Uniquely crotch-accessible, this line of clothing is for any woman planning to step off the porch—hiker or skier, runner or cyclist, boater or farmer, fisherwoman or cowgirl. Overlapping pull-apart layers or front-to-back zippers go beyond any conventional thinking in women's activewear. I can remember trips to the grocery story when I could have used these pants. The Outdoor Woman continues to cater to women who poop and pee in the woods, offering summer shorts, thermal Long Jans (after Janice), slacks, coveralls, and bibs. Anderson has kept Morgan's motto: Never be caught with your pants down! (**The Outdoor Woman** • www.theoutdoorwoman.net • 41313 London Drive • Parker, CO 80138 • Phone: 209-456-6603 • Email: janice@theoutdoorwoman.net)

It's also possible to master a stand-up peeing technique clothed in a pair of standard loose-fitting shorts by sliding the crotch material to one side. One friend does this and then squats, but another woman I know can adjust the material and then stand right along a roadside to pee. If, in driving by, you miss seeing her stream, you might guess she was only stretching her legs and soaking up the view. Practice is the secret, they say. I am going to practice.

For now, back to wearing shorts, jeans, and bikini underwear, wherein the process of peeing usually becomes limited to sitting or squatting. Squatting was never one of my best shots; the liquid soon puddled up and spattered onto everything within three feet. In addition, I have a lousy sense of balance. With all muscles in tight concentration, my success at relaxing the few correct ones to facilitate peeing without toppling over was comparable to my luck on the slot machines: jackpot once in a lifetime.

Slowly, I recognized that after years of conditioning, I couldn't pee if I couldn't relax, and I couldn't relax if I couldn't sit. So with squatting essentially out of the picture, my experimenting narrowed to various approaches to sitting. In my first attempts, I sat on low rocks. This led again to the puddle-up and spatter effect, the only difference being wet thighs instead of wet ankles.

Then came several tries directly on the ground, based on some left-over-from-college-physics notion that proximity decreases velocity—think of pouring lemonade into a pie pan. Direct contact with the earth gave me a thrilling primordial closeness to nature but proved disastrous. Either I ended up sitting in the puddle or, trying a slight incline to avoid that, I wound up with a problem rather like trying to anticipate the flow of Kilauea's lava. How far and in which direction was that steaming stuff going to travel? Usually far enough to wipe out the jeans draped around my feet. Furthermore, leaves, burrs, twigs, and foxtails—all having a tendency to stick to my buns—would lodge themselves in my undergarments, ending up in more critical cracks and crannies.

A few more days of trial and error dampened yet another theory; sitting on higher objects merely encouraged a more direct route into my boots. But I remained undaunted, and enjoying my freedom from walls too much to scurry back to a finely polished, containerized seat, I set off in search of smoother surfaces away from the spray.

Finally, here it is. For those of us whose squatting muscles have atrophied (a mutation that I'm certain paralleled the advent of privy seats), for those of us who didn't grow up on the farm or going fishing with grandpa, and for those of us who wish to experience a piss in the woods with the same high quality of enjoyment one experiences devouring a piece of good New York cheesecake, here is the secret to not peeing in your boots.

First, leave camp in plenty of time to locate an inspiring view far enough into the bush that your urethra won't tie itself into a bowline at the thought of "being seen." Remember: the *can*—the only mental relief available on occasion—acquires its reputation for offering restful respite largely because of its isolation. Now look for a spot with two rocks, or two logs, or a rock and a log close together. Slide your pants down around your ankles and seat yourself near the front edge of one rock. Then prop up your feet—off the ground—on the other. Here you can sit, relax, avoid all showers, and keep sticker free. The steep incline of a hillside, the side of a boulder, or a tree trunk can also be used as the second rock. If you're something of a rock climber, you can actually brace yourself in a narrow passageway between two flat-faced boulders or rock walls (a chimney, climbers call it) with your back flat against one side, your knees slightly bent, and your feet flat against the other. In a desert where there are no rocks or logs, you can still sit instead of squat. Pee from the edge of your pack or bedroll; in sand there will be no splatter.

What's more, if you want to coolly flaunt "this is no sweat for an old hand like me; I was born a frontierswoman," find a two-rock spot behind a boulder or bush (waist high) from where you can casually, with dignity intact, carry on a conversation. Well, maybe not completely intact on the initial try, but be patient. The combination of *women, peeing,* and *dignity* takes a bit of getting used to—not only for you but also for the people with whom you'll be conversing. Be brave. Act "as if" at first; appear nonchalant. Practice. Teach. Be persistent. Eventually, the world will change. And in the meantime, keep your feet up and dry while gazing blissfully over the misty mountaintops in complete peace and satisfaction.

🌿

The other imperative for women traipsing around in the great outdoors is to engineer a discreet, environmental approach to menstruation. You might never feel as brazen as one woman packer I observed stooped over a campfire cooking breakfast for twenty people. Behind her ear, tucked into her sun-blond curls, where one might stick a pencil, she sported a paper-clad tampon, just waiting for a moment's break in the chores. But for most of us twenty-first-century urban women of propriety traveling in the company of others (and also for any of us who'd rather not offer opportunity to attribute our natural assertiveness to being "on the rag"), here is the plan.

First, find a container in which to store your major monthly supply. I've used a metal Band-Aid box or a lovely antique tin.

This size works well for applicatorless tampons. A month's supply fits neatly into the tin, and the tin snugs into the corner of an ammo can, lashed to a raft. When I'm driving a team of horses and my hands stay dirty all day on the trail, I use tampons with applicators. These require a larger container. If you use sanitary pads, you will need one even roomier. The latest designer bag you brought home from boutique shopping, a soft satin travel case, or an old cookie tin all work equally well. This is the main supply and remains stowed away in the depths of your duffel bag or backpack or ammo can.

Next, you need a container for daily use—something to keep handy and slip into your pocket when you stroll off in search of your place of easement. A small cosmetic or ditty bag makes for good camouflage, though an ordinary, clear zip-closing bag will do (some women slap duct tape on the outside). Inside you will keep a day's supply of whatever you're using, some additional bags for storing refuse (used t.p., tampons, sanitary pads, and any paper or cellophane wrappers, all of which *must* be packed out), and a cache of clean t.p. or a pocket packet of tissues. Tissues are a good choice; they can be handed out quite politely to others in need, and the packet can be tucked into a pocket when your day kit becomes jammed. During the day, the refuse bags will reside in your day kit that's stashed in your pocket, a fanny pack, a saddlebag, an ammo can, or an outside pocket of a backpack.

Any fecally soiled t.p. must be collected, stored, and disposed of separately. It can be burned in a campfire or, when you get home, in a woodstove; it can be deposited in a portable toilet or a trailhead vault-type outhouse; or it can be carefully flushed (in average-size wads) down a toilet connected to a septic or sewer system. Choose a washable, reusable bag—perhaps of water-resistant nylon—for stashing your soiled tissue. At evening camp when you resupply your day kit, you'll transfer the refuse into a larger holding bag in your main supply sack. See chapter 4 for the handy solo containers for poop packers. Another simple accessory for outdoor women is a pee rag: usually a bandana or half a bandana, to use for blotting. Tie it, to dry, on the outside of a backpack and rinse it out whenever you come across water.

On organized expeditions, the central garbage is often sorted into burnable and pack-out refuse. To limit the volume and weight of the pack-out garbage, the paper trash is burned in the evening campfire or the last thing before breaking camp. Give what you can to the central garbage. (With a private trip, apprise yourself thoroughly of campfire regulations; open fires are not allowed in many areas or can require burn pans and special ash disposal.) Also keep in mind that tampons and sanitary napkins need a hot fire to be completely consumed. Once, when I was a novice in my newly acquired environmental awareness, I returned to camp under cover of darkness and surreptitiously slipped a small carefully wadded bundle into the coals. While we drank Swiss Miss, sang songs, and exchanged flip and wrap stories, to my horror, the fire slowly blackened and peeled away only the wrappings of my gift. The safest thing to do on a group outing is to ask the trip leader or one of the guides about disposal procedures.

After all this, the Enema Man's approach begins to sound pretty good. I can only suggest one thing to help. Think of the days when you're utterly depressed from hearing about desperate situations of people and environments around the world—situations you wish you might change, but there seems to be nothing you can do. Then think about how easy it is—really—to pack out soiled tissue. Mother Earth will yodel "thank you," and you will know you've actually made a difference for one tiny moment in time. Until it becomes routine, you might have to approach it this way. I still often do.

🌱

Now for a word, or a great bunch of words, on transformative feminine funnels, or FUDs (female urinary devices). These articles to facilitate a woman's peeing come in disposable waterproof cardboard or washable reusable plastic, or silicone, and should by rights be available in every public toilet. With slight variations in shape, the principle is the same for all models. The funnel, elongated and elliptical, affords a comfortable fit between a woman's legs and allows her to direct her stream. It adds a convenient frontal attack to grandmother's stand-up peeing style, is handy for cramped restrooms (say, in airplanes), yucky-looking toilet seats, landscapes with no cover, and even traffic jams. FUDs have been put to good use in convalescent hospitals, and they're a boon to active women in wheelchairs. Elderly women and pregnant women use them. A woman in a body cast employed one; a woman with a hip replacement loved hers. Marathon runners, pilots, and women in the military adore theirs. It was years ago that I first saw funnels advertised in *Latitude 38*, a marine publication. They were delighting women sailors who wanted to avoid going below in order to *go*—a ship's cramped head being the worst spot to hang out if you're prone to seasickness. The funnel entailed no dropping of drawers, only an unzipping of shorts or pulling aside of a bathing suit. Women could stand tall—hip to hip with the men—and pee over the rail. Now FUDS have found homes with women mountain climbers, bicyclists, sea kayakers, festival-goers, pub crawlers, and big game hunters. Even motorcycle mamas. I've met traveling women who've carried theirs on trains, ferries, and buses all over the world. No more staying dehydrated for fear of having to pee!

My initial excitement about funnels was in the thought they might be precisely the solution for sleeping out on nippy nights. With a hose, I might pee at 4:00 a.m. without having to crawl out of my toasty bag. Upon first use, one disadvantage became immediately apparent. The longest of the hoses (and you need the longest in this situation) tends to have a strongly coiled memory. With persistence I could stretch it out, but let go and the end flipped around to spray everything in sight like an out-of-control fire hose. In addition, if I expected the liquid to exit the correct end, I had to remember the principle of gravity. Having gone to the trouble of hunting up a perfectly flat spot on which to bed, I had to work hard to stay within the warmth of my bedroll while rising enough to provide a downhill flow. Although I have reports from women who manage this well, I say forget it! A few moments of scampering about in the frost makes me all the more appreciative of a warm bag—just part of the daily allotment of minor inconveniences and miseries that seem to help me retain a healthy and humble perspective on life. Finally, if you're inside a tent with sleet pelting the sides, try coupling the funnel with a collector bag or bottle.

For those of us being dragged, kicking and screaming, into the twenty-first century, the old coffee can routine works just fine.

It's for cross-country skiing, to my mind, that the funnel becomes indispensable, for when the charming outhouse is a couple miles off and I'm sporting layers of clothing. I'll slip one into a zip-closing bag (though some funnels come with a case) and keep it tucked in an accessible pocket. Then, once again, like the men, I can step a dozen feet off the trail and turn my back. With a full bladder, I can even write my name! (But leave no sign, cover over that yellow snow.) The funnel has cut my pee time from sometimes forty-five minutes to three. Previously, I'd been skiing off into woods that provide little cover when the ground is a startling white, plowing through knee-deep snow to scout a spot, then skinning down pants and long johns and trying hopelessly to squat between my skis, which would invariably pop my bindings. Digging out was such an exhausting hassle that I often considered lying down and freezing over 'til spring.

For anyone interested in experimenting with a funnel, the investment will be small. And *do* experiment, in the shower or backyard. Tilting forward at the hips or dropping the level of the FUD's exit hole will help the pee flow down and out. If you have a forceful flow, you can snip back the end on many of these, like you would the nib of a cake-frosting bag. Try sealing the funnel tight against the body or giving it a little room to breathe, especially in the front; every woman's anatomy is uniquely her own. Use the back edge of the funnel to catch the last drips. And, to avoid a warm, wet surprise, make sure the little bugger is fairly well empty before removing it. Urine is sterile as it exits the body— unless you have a bladder infection, and this you would know.

Funnels, in recent years, have blossomed into a colorful bouquet of products, to the extent that you can color-coordinate or make a personal fashion statement. They sell to numerous joyous tunes: "no more tush in the bush," "female freedom," "don't take life sitting down," "stand up and take control," "banish bare bottoms," "because life's greatest adventure shouldn't be finding a restroom." So select your ditty and get weeing.

Listed in the order of my acquaintance. (Visit their wonderful websites.)

Washable, Reusable FUDs

Freshette ■ www.freshette.com ■ International Sani-fem Company ■ P.O. Box 4117 ■ Downey, CA 90241 ■ Phone in U.S.: 800-542-5580; outside U.S. 562-928-3435 ■ Email: sanifem@aol.com

The Sports & Travel Freshette Package ($23.95) includes a pink plastic FUD, or olive drab for the military, a 5-inch extension tube, and a zippered travel pouch. Extension Tubes come in 36- and 48-inch lengths, or custom cut. Collector Bags ($12.95 for a 12-pack).

SHEWEE ■ www.shewee.com ■ 49 Walton Street ■ Walton on the Hill, KT20 7RR UK ■ Phone toll-free in UK: 0844-800-8270; from U.S. +44 (0) 1737819400 ■ Email: info@shewee.com

The SHEWEE funnel ($14.95) is available in fuchsia, brilliant blue, and clear molded plastic. The SHEWEE Extreme ($22.95) includes a 5-inch extension for use with bulky clothing, and a carrying case. Extension Tube by itself ($2.95); Carrying Case ($7.95); Absorbent Pouch collector bags ($10 for 2-pack). SHEWEE also offers X-fronts ($20), women's shorty boxers in fuchsia with "fly" front for funnel access and a waistband emblazoned with STAND UP AND TAKE CONTROL! Click on USA flag for shipping from a U.S. distributor.

BioRelief.com ■ www.biorelief.com/sports-fans.html ■ 5610 NW 12th Avenue, Suite 214 ■ Fort Lauderdale, FL 33309 ■ Phone: 877-782-3675 ■ Email: info@biorelief.com

BioRelief offers the Lady J ($9.95), a light blue plastic funnel, which is also the woman's adapter for the Little John ($12.95), a flat-bottomed red jug. The Travel John ($6.49 for a 3-pack) has a unisex adaptor as part of a plastic bag. The Stadium Gal ($34.95)

is equipped with a leg hose and calf bag for the party-hardy wishing to bypass restroom lines at concerts, athletic events, or Mardi Gras. Many other items are available, including a flexible soft plastic commode seat (folds in half) with a groove for a 5-gallon bucket—sit on it and it seals.

GoGirl ■ **www.go-girl.com** ■ FemMed Inc. ■ 11601 Minnetonka Mills Road, Suite F ■ Minnetonka, MN 55305 ■ Phone: 877-447-5007 ■ Email: CustomerService@go-girl.com

The GoGirl funnel ($9.99 with carrying tube; $26.97 for 3-pack) is made of flexible, medical-grade silicone (can withstand boiling) and has a built-in splash guard. Available in lavender or khaki. Comes rolled up in a carrying tube with a tissue and baggie. Dries quickly—wash 'em or toss 'em!

TravelMate ■ **www.whenyagottago.com** ■ Shalin, Inc. ■ 4347 North Alderbrook Drive ■ Coeur d'Alene, ID 83815 ■ Phone: 208-691-9524 ■ Email: linda@whenyagottago.com

The TravelMate ($7.95; $21 for 3-pack) is sky-blue plastic; its handle and cradle together are about the size of a dainty cigar, making it the smallest I've seen. The cradle fits *between* the folds of the outer lips (labia majora) and covers the inner lips (labia minora) and the urethra's opening. Follow the directions for positioning and adjust the handle to a downward angle. TravelMates are used for stand-up peeing or, with various thermoplastic tubing and collection bags, employed while seated. Clean with soap and water or the alcohol-free HandClens ($2.95 for 5 ounces), a sanitizing spritzer. Also available: Tapestry Carrying Case ($7.25) and Magic Towels ($1.25 for box of 8). The latter are miniscule handwipes—imagine two Tums, stacked—which, with a couple drops of water, balloon into a reusable towel. Disposable Magic Cones ($3.95 for 3-pack; $10 for three 3-packs) are flat-folded biodegradable funnels of waterproofed cardboard that pop open into lock position when squeezed.

Disposable FUDS

GoGirl and **TravelMate GoGirl** (see page 94)

P-MATE ■ **www.pmateusa.com** ■ Phone: 720-317-3303 ■ Email: info@pmateusa.com

The P-MATE ($4.95 for 5-pack) is a single-use "Stand-to-pee Device" of form-fashioned cardboard. Flat-folded, it pops open. Comes in widely colorful designs. Available online from distributors in Israel, Germany, UK, Canada, and U.S.

Uri-Mate Protector ■ **www.uri-mate.com** ■ Uri-Mate Head Office ■ 32 Hartley Road ■ London, E11 3BL, UK ■ Phone: 786-317-6254 ■ Email: info@uri-mate.com

The Uri-Mate Protector ($9.95 for 5-pack, 3 cones to a pack) is a biodegradable, thin cardboard cone. Comes in a cellophane packet, a smidgeon larger and flatter than a teabag, with a sweet pink rose graphic. Just unfold. Instructions in English and Spanish. Available online from distributors in UK, U.S., and Venezuela.

❧

In closing this chapter and to warm your hearts, I pass along the following story related to me by an employee of a Sausalito yachting supply house:

> *After carefully selecting a pink plastic funnel, an elderly white-haired couple arrived at the cash register, whereupon the woman demurely inquired whether a longer hose might be attached for her. Her request was gladly granted and the funnel whisked away to the back workroom. Then, lifting her gentle, wisdom-aged face toward her husband, with a cherubic wink she crooned, "Now, dear, mine will be longer than yours!"*

7 What? No T.P.? or Doing Without

Back to the Pleistocene

—Earth First! bumper sticker

Conjure up for a moment one of those predawn suburban mornings when you emerge reluctantly from the warm bedding and bump along the walls to the bathroom, to sit, just another shadow, hunched on the bowl. Eyes shut against the real world, elbows dug into knees, and chin settled in a cradle of knuckles, you are soon drowsily appreciating the serenity following a particularly portly poop. Then, wishing you could beam yourself back to horizontal again, you blindly grope for the toilet paper only to find your fingertips spinning a naked cylinder of cardboard, sending up the flapping racket of a pinwheel. Rats! You're forced to flip on all one hundred watts, stumble across the room to the cabinet under the sink, and fish out and unwrap a new roll. You might exchange it for the empty one (if you were truly a good person), but the dexterity involved would require your final emergence from dreamland.

Or how about this: It's one of those ghastly, highfalutin dinner parties—not casual, not just old friends. It could be a Waterford and Limoges setting at the elderly boss's estate or maybe the new girlfriend's esteemed literary family all gathered to look you over. The seven-course meal has been consumed, yet the formality of intercourse has not relaxed. As a matter of fact, the guests are perched around the ornate living room like so many stately, stoic great blue herons, picking quietly at thin-layered desserts and sipping tea. Suddenly, amid all this propriety, the spiced prune conserve which had accompanied the main course and is now somewhere south of your stomach, screams at you to leap up and excuse yourself—politely, of course, on the pretense of helping (the kitchen staff?) with the dishes.

Once into the hallway, with downward-pointed toes lifted high in double time, you detour to the powder room in a perfect rendition of Sylvester the Cat. Shortly thereafter comes the discovery that your hostess has neglected to renew the supply of toilet paper, which—unbeknownst to you—she keeps in the hall closet. You've finished crawling through all the cupboards: now what? Do you hobble to the door with your pants around your knees, poke your nose through the crack, and coolly call, *psst*? Whenever someone disappears into the bathroom at a party, others imagine her/him preening before the mirror, checking for spinach between the teeth, "freshening up," or—possibly— tinkling. Straining and pooping? Never. But all pretenses go out the window when you holler for toilet paper (in a pinch, even a woman will drip-dry number one). For the rest of the evening you might as well wear a sandwich board with three-foot headlines proclaiming what you've been up to.

Next is the classic Gas Station Mad Dash: surely there isn't a person in the First World who's escaped this one. It begins with the feverish circling of the facility in an effort to park nearest the doors with the stick-figure emblems. Either one that's empty is fair game in emergencies. Somehow you manage to climb out of your vehicle; dance across the pavement in a doubled-over version of the cowboy *schottische* (inspired by constricted sphincter muscles) and throw open the restroom door—oh, miracle of miracles!—without having to humiliate yourself by begging for a key. But there your good fortune ends. Almost immediately you realize the only scraps of toilet paper are flotsam on the lake in which you're standing, there isn't a shred of tissue in any of your pockets, and the paper towel dispenser is "Jeez, why me?" empty.

For pure perspective, I'll recount the above stories, or equally painful paperless scenarios, when people respond to the idea of experimenting in the woods without t.p. as though they'd fallen into a vat of putrefying fish guts. There's nothing so disgusting about it, really.

As with all major changes, adjusting to the absence of that readily available soft quilted white stuff wound neatly 'round a cylinder takes a bit of getting used to. Once it has been successfully maneuvered, however, scrubbing one's posterior with a snatch of biodegradable nature is a noteworthy experience, whereupon one's ecologically prescribed place in the universe can come vividly into focus. Puffed up with pride, or jubilant with primitive freedom, one might be startled to hear a rousing chorus of approval from the forest fairies. So I've been told.

Doing without toilet paper takes me back, way back. Mr. Neanderthal might have had skin like horsehide and needn't have bothered with wiping, but I swear I can sense ghostly forms—him and his buddies—lurking about, curious, every time I walk away from a purely organic burial of shit and leaves. After an accomplishment of this sort, I'll bounce along absurdly pleased with myself, a euphoric little note within a great harmony. Such mysterious brushes with my deepest origins not only overwhelm but also refresh me, as tangibly as a hot shower after a week of mountain sweat and dirt. All at once I feel powerfully attached to a cosmic whole, simple in an age of complexity, perfectly in tune with the world, yet tiny and humble, and, of all things, enchantingly ancient. Vats of putrefying fish guts—phooey!

Be it a personal quest to function as simply as the primeval wandering tribes, or a feeling of bliss at not having to pack around rolls of bulky tissue and bags of carry-out garbage—whatever your motivation, here are a few suggestions to get your started. The library is not full of pertinent references to t.p. alternatives, and I will never have covered enough ground to have all the answers. You will have to depart from the text after finishing this chapter and experiment on your own. Call it scientific research.

When I began my evaluation of leaves, I remembered my dear old high school friend Jan who once traveled across Europe keeping a toilet paper diary, replete with sample bits from different countries. She returned to the States with everything from pieces of brown wrapping paper to wax paper and shrink-wrap. Is it, I wonder, worth speculating on the regional correlations between indigenous plant leaves and present-day toilet paper quality? If you think you have trouble selecting brands in the supermarket, wait until you see the spectrum nature has to offer.

A vast assortment, some obviously more appropriate to the task than others, are yours for the picking. But wait. A few words of caution are necessary:

There are many wildland items suitable for natural toilet paper, and the choice of living plants should only be a last resort. If you pick leaves at all, be especially mindful. Always select dead grasses and leaves over live ones. Don't pick wildflowers or rare species. Don't pick in parks or other restricted areas. Don't pull anything up by the roots. Don't rob large clumps or strip entire branches. Carefully pick a leaf here, a leaf there—so no one, not even the plant (especially the plant), will know you have been there. In the following pages you will find many suggestions for nonliving t.p. substitutes.

To hunt leaves, an introductory course in botany is not necessary; neither must you learn every leaf by name. But engrave in your memory poison oak, poison ivy, poison sumac, and those sneaky stinging nettles, all illustrated in any good field guide. A dinner date with Frankenstein's monster or the Wicked Witch of the West would be a joyous interlude compared to the aftermath of using one of those devils on your keister. Should you be seriously planning to hang out with my Neanderthaloid apparitions and also be a member of the species I call Exotic Trekkies (those who roam about in out-of-the-way climes), then read up on the vegetation native to the areas you plan to visit, to ascertain whether some peculiar variety of poison pine or viperous honeysuckle ought to be added to your don't-touch list.

When leafstalking, look for the large and the soft. Mullein leaves are a favorite: soft, cushy, almost woolly, and one leaf will do. Thimbleberry is another large-leafed plant and praiseworthy once you discover the soft side opposite the slick. Plants with small or palmated leaves can be used by the handful (remember —one here, one there). Frequently, there will be no perfect specimen available. At those times, the profusion and ample diameters of leaves such as California's wild grape can offer compensation for their waxy slickness.

Before picking, be sure to examine leaves carefully; they sometimes can be *sticky* (as though covered by a thin layer of syrup), *scabrous* (having a rasplike surface), annoyingly *prickly* owing to small bristles and barbs or, more seriously, *hispidulous* (covered with sharp hairs stiff enough to penetrate the skin). Stay away from reeds, bamboo, and some grasses—in effect, slicing leaves—that can cause agonizing wounds like paper cuts. With a little attention, you'll learn which ones to avoid and be on your way to becoming a connoisseur of fine leaves.

Autumn woodlands—not to be shamed by the swankiest powder room décor—offer us a leaf selection in vibrant designer shades. Not all fallen leaves dry and crumble immediately. In some climates, many will stay pliable through the winter months. Alpine winters, where deciduous vegetation is scarce, can be a bit of a problem. For a matter of months in many parts of the high country, evergreens are the only selection. Draw on your creativity. Dried pine needles can be put to good use, provided you have the time to line them all up in the same direction. The odd stick on the ground might be useful, if it's smooth and you remember to rub with the grain. Foresters of the Northwest are partial to something I've always known to make great Halloween handlebar mustaches—the dark brown *Bryoria* lichen that hangs abundantly from trees in long gauzy streamers. There's also the yellowish green *Alectoria*. And pinecones are reputedly good tools, but steer clear of the spiky rotund cones and stick with the narrow, softer, aging ones. A world-renowned river rafter of my acquaintance swears by old spongy Douglas fir cones.

My cross-country skiing partner promotes snowballs as the perfect winter wipe—that is, once you brace yourself for the momentary shock. Try it. To me, the freeze is a minor trauma compared to visiting one of those inglorious chemical toilets that sit, invariably in the sun, on construction sites and at festivals, exuding gagging aromas from the contents cooking within.

Let us return to the exalted woods. In your rummaging in the great outdoors for t.p.–like items, you're bound to find many suitable materials. Try sheets of smooth peeling bark, polished driftwood, seashells, and large feathers. Steer clear of mosses; they're fragile, shouldn't be disturbed, and crumble uselessly anyway.

In the rural areas of many countries, there are people who have never laid eyes on toilet paper. In parts of the Middle East, a person carries a wet cloth into the fields. The custom of religiously eating with the right hand was not born of divine Arab vision but of prudent hygiene: the left hand wiped. I wouldn't want to discourage you if this particular system works for you, but before settling on it permanently, you might consider that for environmental reasons (discussed in chapter 2) this method will entail carrying, along with a cloth, two small buckets for washing and rinsing. The second bucket is used for rinsing out the first, to avoid dipping the fecally contaminated wash bucket directly into wilderness water. Afterward, bury the wash and rinse water well away from any watercourse.

There exists another paperless technique, but it seldom emerges as an option with our persnickety Western ways, which seem to require by cultural edict keeping copious wads between our fingertips and our bums. This approach comes to us mostly by way of Old World countries and from one well-traveled family physician, Dr. Charles Helm, who was born in South Africa and made his way to remote northern British Columbia to set up his practice. We'll call it the *water wipe*.

Nothing is needed but a container for water: a canteen, a cup, a cook pot, and a hat have all been suggested. Fill your container and carry it to your chosen spot. Then, squatting over your one-sit hole, trickle water from the container into your free hand—never contaminating the fresh water—and use it to splash or wipe. This trickling procedure poses no problem for agile squatters and adept skateboarders, but, having been born minus a balance gene, I find it a difficult maneuver. Almost as efficient as trickling is the repeated moistening of one hand, customarily the left.

The water wipe has definite pluses. For the minimalist, it saves on space and weight—both carry-in and carry-out—and it saves trees (used t.p. is not recycled). Unless you're in terrain short on water, the water wipe becomes the ideal wipe. (Tissue can still be carried for instances of traveler's trots.) Don't forget to wash your hands.

Dr. Helm takes the whole matter to yet another level by suggesting if we were to model our diets more after that of horses, we might dispense altogether with wiping, being able ourselves to "neatly pinch off" road apples. A healthy human, Helm believes, need not carry *bogroll* (*bog* is a South African euphemism for bathroom) in the wilderness, though he admits "the fastidious and prudish amongst our number will not be impressed with a blanket ban on bogroll in the bush."

In a long letter, he goes on with his thoughts:

> *Have you ever watched a horse shit? . . . the process begins with a fart by way of preamble, followed by a voluntary relaxation of the anal sphincter, the passage of a number of well-formed, not-too-hard, not-too-soft turds, then a gentle, well-coordinated contraction . . . [whence the whole] falls to the ground without any of its substance remaining adhered to the horse. The entire process is easy, efficient, and above all has no need of toilet paper.*
>
> *Our Western diets have wreaked havoc with our bowel regularity, leading to stools of varying consistency and a consequent increased need for bogroll. We have not only lost the art of shitting in the woods, we have lost the art of shitting, period. Perhaps it is related to the innate fear of being caught with a turd half-in and half-out, but your average mortal will constrict that sphincter as soon as a respectable fraction has seen the light of day. No turd can withstand this kind of strangulation, and inevitably the distal portion breaks off, the proximal part remains put, and a substantial segment close to the sphincter gets smeared all over. I suspect that most humans tighten that dread sphincter half a dozen times per crap. And the bogroll industry gloats and smirks.*

There's definitely something to be said in this regard for a meatless, high-fiber diet.

Arid, sandy terrains are the most critically lacking in t.p. substitutes. In a dry creek bed you can sometimes find a smooth, sun-baked stone—state-of-the-art wipe! But beware. Under a blazing sun, stones can gather enough BTUs to brand cattle. Before using a stone, test it in your hand, then on your wrist as you would the milk in a baby's bottle. And remember not to return a soiled stone to the creek bed.

There you have it: all I know today.

Hmmm. Well, I once met a man who proposed that I curry my bum with sand in the mountain man's age-old manner of scouring pots and pans. But I have a hunch this curmudgeonly old bugger was, or had, like my own Mr. N., a horse-hide's ass. Me, I'll stick to snowballs and stones.

Now you're on your own.

Definition of Shit

¹**shit** /'shit/ *vb* **shit** *or* **shat** \\'shat\\; **shit-ting** [alter. (Influenced by ²shit and the past and pp. forms) of earlier *shite*, fr. ME *shiten*, fr. OE

scítan; akin to MLG & MD *schîten* to defecate, OHG *scízan*, MHG schizan, ON *skíta* to defecate, OE *scēadon* to divide or separate—more at SHED] *v.i.* 1. to defecate; often used figuratively to express embarrassment <I thought I'd ~ when I had to pee and there wasn't any place to hide>. or fear <I just about ~ when I stepped off the ski lift and viewed the hill from above>. ~ *v.t.* to defecate something <~ watery stools>. 2. to fool, to mislead, to put on <You wouldn't ~ me about using pinecones for toilet paper, would you?>.

shit bricks; 1. to worry. 2. to be terrified.

shit can; 1. to throw away. 2. to ban. 3. to fire or dismiss.

shit fruit salad (also: shit nickels, shit ice cream); said of a prima donna <She's so special, she must ~>.

shit on; 1. to ruin, to muck up. 2. to treat unfairly, often by being extremely rude or unkind or harsh.

shit oneself; 1. to defile oneself with excrement. 2. to deceive oneself.

shit the bed; 1. to foul your nest, to stupidly mess up your own good situation. 2. to die.

²**shit** \\'shit\\ *n.* [fr. (assumed) ME, fr. OE *scite* (attested only in place names); akin to MD *schit, schitte* excrement, OE *scitan* to defecate] 1. a: feces b: garbage; junk; unorganized or unrelated articles, stuff <Never leave ~ in the woods>. 2. lies, nonsense, exaggeration <a bunch of ~>. 3. to know nothing <we didn't know ~ about poop-packing>.

a shit; derogatory term.

bad shit; a consumable of piss-poor quality; generally refers to street drugs.

big shit; someone with an overinflated sense of self-importance.

blow (a person's) shit away; to kill; figuratively, to astound.

built like a brick shit house; well built.

bullshit; 1. lies, nonsense. 2. trash; useless junk. 3. name of a group word game. 4. an interjection of fierce disagreement.

chickenshit; n. 1. a coward. 2. petty behavior. *adj.* cowardly.

crock of shit; something false or deceptive <Campaign promises are usually a ~>.

deep shit; big trouble; also stated *knee-deep in shit.*

dipshit; idiot, nerd.

dish out shit; to deliver reprimands or punishment; also, to abuse verbally.

Do bears shit in the woods?; rhetorical reply to statement of the obvious.

doesn't know shit from Shinola; can't tell the difference between excrement and brown shoe polish.

dogshit; 1. low-down, dirty, trashed-out. 2. interjection expressing hot disapproval.

Don't give me that shit! ; 1. shut up. 2. don't kid me.

dumbshit; a pathetic incompetent.

eat sawdust and shit 2x4s; 1. meaning to overwork. 2. meaning overly competent <She can ~>.

eat shit; 1. to lose a game by a large margin. 2. to get a very raw deal; to absorb or withstand many insults over even physical abuse. 3. to humble oneself. 4. an angry demand, meaning to go away, or drop dead.

get your shit together; 1. undergo great personal growth; to become organized or focused. 2. admonition to hurry up.

good shit; a product of excellent quality or flavor; generally a reference to street drugs.

Holy shit!; exclamation of surprise, discovery, realization, or fear.

horseshit; 1. lies, double-talk. 2. interjection of vehement disagreement.

hot shit; a class act; a popular item; frequently used sarcastically <Just because he climbed Everest, he thinks he's ~>.

jack shit; a negative value; to do *jack shit* is to do less than nothing.

know your shit; to be an expert in your field.

little shit; 1. person of small stature; petty annoyance. 2. term of endearment for someone who is looked upon admiringly as a sweet rascal.

No shit?; 1. exclamation ranging from high excitement to surprise; often similar to *Really?*; used sarcastically in response to something already known. 2. exclamation of hearty agreement.

Oh, shit!; exclamation of surprise or disgust; when pronounced \oo shit\ generally a warning of impending doom; can also mean *Whoops!;* when pronounced \o shee' it\ indicates great pain or embarrassment, or a colossal disaster; when pronounced \aw shit\ expresses regret or sympathy or shyness.

old shit; things or ideas that have become outmoded; behavior patterns that no longer work; old baggage or agendas.

piece of shit; 1. cheaply constructed article. 2. bad person.

scare the living shit out of; terrorize.

shit; also \shee-y-it\ (emphatic form) exclamation of annoyance < Well, ~ ! I peed my pants>.

shitburgers; exclamation of dismay.

shitcan; toilet; garbage can; honey bucket.

shit-eating grin; smile of overt satisfaction.

shit happens; expresses the sentiment "the best-laid plans often go awry"; often seen on bumper stickers.

shit hits the fan; 1. violent or unpleasant situation, often in reference to reprimands coming down from authority figures. 2. major organizational shake-up.

Shit, man! /sheet män/; 1. generic expression for surprise, disgust, delight, or anger. 2. expression of pleasure, appreciation, or astonishment.

shit on a brick; exclamation of great disgust.

shit on a shingle; creamed chipped beef on toast.

shit on wheels; 1. someone who gets a lot done. 2. a holy terror. 3. a braggart who nevertheless carries it off.

shit or get off the pot; quit wasting time or stalling; make a decision.

shit out of luck; having ill fortune.

shoot the shit; to engage in friendly conversation.

stay out of my shit; admonition to mind your own business, to stop meddling.

sure as shit; a very definite and sometimes predictable occurrence; true to form.

take a shit; to defecate.

take shit; to accept abuse or ridicule.

the shits; 1. diarrhea. 2. a dreary, rotten situation <Camping in this cold, damp cave full of bats is ~>.

tough shit; 1. expression indicating bad luck, similar to *Too bad!* or *That's the way the cookie crumbles!* 2. angry response, stronger than *So what!*

up shit's creek; in a bad situation.

shitaree *n*. a toilet; portable potty; something one shits into.

shit-ass *n*. a reprehensible individual.

shit-bird *n*. a mild, sometimes half-affectionate name for a scoundrel.

shit-brain *n*. an idiot.

shit burgers *interj*. mild exclamation of disgust or disappointment.

shit disturber *n*. an instigator.

shit-faced *adj*. drunk or otherwise intoxicated.

shit-fire *n*. a mean, nasty person; a bully.

shit-fit *n*. a temper tantrum; a tizzy.

shit-head *n*. halfway between a shit-ass and a shit-bird.

shit-hole *n*. 1. a: a toilet b: the hole in the privy board; often used figuratively <Financing the research for a biodegradable bag for packing-it-out would not be throwing money down the ~>. 2. the anus. 3. undesirable place.

shit-house *n.* 1. a bathroom or an outhouse.

in the shit house; in disrepute.

shit-house poet; 1. anyone who scribbles graffiti on restroom walls; 2. a lousy poet.

shitless, *adj.* state of extreme fear <scared ~>.

shit list *n.* a figurative list, implies persons held in low esteem <The person who forgot to pack the toilet paper is on everyone's ~>.

shit load *n.* big, huge, behemoth.

shit-put *n.* the act of jumping in saltwater for an overboard defecation from a sea kayak; also called an *aqua-dump*.

shit shark *n.* the person who operates the honey wagon.

shit storm *n.* 1. a fiery response, as in emotional eruption; 2. an actual barrage of weaponry.

shitter *n.* an outhouse; a toilet.

in the shitter; in disrepute.

shitter time; a place to think things out; discipline in a drug rehab program.

shitty /shit-ē/ *adj.*, **shit-ti-er, -est** 1. inept. 2. inferior quality, cheap, bad, or ugly; denotes a state of being that is somehow dreadful, often as a result of physical pain or guilt <My pee ran right down that little mole's hole and now I feel ~>.

Afterword

We need to foster a bosom friendship with land and water and air. I did not once write the word *wilderness* in these pages without some cringing and self-evaluation. I remember the telling words of Chief Luther Standing Bear of the Oglala Sioux:

> *We did not think of the great open plains, the beautiful rolling hills, and winding streams with tangled growth, as "wild." Only to the white man was nature a "wilderness" and only to him was the land "infested" with "wild" animals and "savage" people. To us it was tame. Earth was bountiful and we were surrounded with the blessings of the Great Mystery. Not until the hairy man from the east came and with brutal frenzy heaped injustices upon us and the families we loved was it "wild" for us. When the very animals of the forest began fleeing from his approach, then it was that for us the "Wild West" began.*

About the Author

A longtime outdoorswoman and river guide, Kathleen Meyer was the founding editor of *Headwaters*, published by Friends of the River. Her *Barefoot Hearted: A Wild Life Among Wildlife* is a Wild West adventure memoir. Kathleen makes her home with Patrick McCarron in Montana's Bitterroot Valley. Visit the author at her website: www.KathleenintheWoods.net.